GW00374678

TAKE ONE SURVEYOR

Take One Surveyor

*An Autobiography by Rafe Clutton, Fellow of
the Royal Institution of Chartered Surveyors*

The Memoir Club

© Rafe Clutton 2004

First published in 2004 by
The Memoir Club
Stanhope Old Hall
Stanhope
Weardale
County Durham

All rights reserved.
Unauthorised duplication
contravenes existing laws.

British Library Cataloguing in
Publication Data.
A catalogue record for this book
is available from the
British Library.

ISBN: 1 84104 098 3

Typeset by George Wishart & Associates, Whitley Bay.
Printed by CPI Bath.

To all at Cluttons, who have given me so much support and loyalty, and above all to Jill, who has, as always, made everything possible.

Contents

Illustrations

Introduction

MY ORIGINAL intention was to write down, while I still remembered them, how the times appeared to a child growing up before and during the war years in a country home in Sussex and in the company of a large and entertaining family. I then found that, without bordering on the tedious, this was hardly enough for even a modest book – at least, not given the limits of my literary abilities. I therefore have gone on to describe something of my life as a partner in the surveying firm, the origins of which go back to my three greats Clutton grandfather. I realize that the first part may, I flatter myself, have appeal to one reader and the latter be the main interest of another. I can only hope that the story as a whole may nevertheless be at least moderately readable.

So many relatives, friends and former colleagues who come into this short history, either directly or indirectly, are no longer available to say whether their recollection of events is the same as mine. To those still with us who may read it I can only say that I have followed my memory as best I can, but if their remembrance of events differs from mine I hope that they will forgive the failings of age. It is not my business to talk of my former clients' affairs, nor should I intrude upon the lives of my family, who should be left to decide, in time, whether or not they wish to tell their own stories. References to clients are therefore only as seems necessary to me to explain my own part in their service and are all now well in the past tense so far as actions and decisions are concerned. My family, I know, will not take my reluctance to intrude, in print, upon their own right to privacy as indicating any lack of the enormous pride that Jill and I take in each and every one of them.

CHAPTER 1

Beginnings

MY FIRST IMPRESSION of our new home was of imminent disaster. Our mother had driven us down a narrow, winding and, at least for those of us in the back seats, distinctly bumpy lane until there came into view a large stone house, under a tiled roof, standing on a rise a little way back from a murky looking pond. This pond became the immediate cause of my concern as my mother had evidently decided to stop at this point so that we could cover the last few rutted yards on foot. That meant turning the car round in the space available between the water on our right, a slope down to some cart sheds on the left, and deep wheel ruts at the approach to a field gate ahead. It was on the second or third run back in this limited space for turning that we came very near to descending into the pond, which was unfenced and bounded only by logs set into the roadside at the same level as the track. Our travel arrangements were such that I was the one nearest to, and best positioned to see, the danger, and my yell of alarm, I like to think, came just in time.

The family car was what was known as a Morris Fourteen and our mode of travel would not have impressed the road safety experts of a later age. My mother combined driving with being a guide to objects of local interest, which often meant that her eyes were rather less on the road than they should have been. Beside her sat our nurse, Sybil, with the baby, my brother Nigel, on her knee. In between the front seats a stool was placed over the back of the hand brake handle and one of my younger sisters, Angela or Marigold, or I would be seated on it. On this occasion it was probably Angela, who was five, as I was in the back and Marigold was only three and too young then not to be on someone's lap. That left my two older sisters, Iris and Shirley, to occupy the back seat, one holding our youngest sister, and with me between them, on this occasion kneeling on the seat and looking out of the back window. Thus I was in a position, I like to think, to save our expedition from a damp conclusion.

My father seldom accompanied us on family outings. For one thing the car was already somewhat crowded but, more particularly, a series of war wounds had culminated in his right leg being amputated above the knee during the Ypres battles of 1917. This meant that he did not drive and much preferred to stay at his gardening hobby than face the discomforts, for him, of squashing up in the car or coping with the country picnics that our mother loved and which were, in the summer months at least, the easiest way in which to feed us all on such occasions. What else happened on that first visit to the house that was to be our family home through the war years and beyond I cannot now remember, but our move shortly afterwards, in May 1936 and just before my seventh birthday, was to prove to be the start of a wonderful country childhood, full of fun, interest and not a little humour.

Before that, I have a few memories of the house at Warlingham where I was born – still there when I last went to look and with the same name on the front gate – but my first real recollections are of my paternal grandmother's home at Balcombe, to which my parents were obliged to move when I was three because my grandmother had been left alone following the elopement of one of my aunts with the gardener; the other unmarried aunt having already left home to live with a friend elsewhere in the village. My grandmother was thus by herself in her large house and demanded company. She had been a hospital sister, nursing my grandfather when he was a patient, and becoming his third wife when he was fifty two and with no surviving child from his earlier marriages. She moved to Balcombe after her husband died in 1927. My parents must have made quite a sacrifice in leaving their Warlingham home and moving the whole family to a house that was not theirs to control. She made little, if any, alteration to her domestic routine, continuing to run the house and her cook and other staff to her customary and rigid standards. My sister Angela and I were installed in a room allocated as the nursery and in the care of a nurse, while our older sisters, then aged nine and eleven, were sent to school in Haywards Heath. Our mother was permitted to do very little of what had filled her day in her former home and she spent the time, when she was not driving my father and sisters to Haywards Heath railway station or school, partly by playing her violin in a nearby orchestra and in bearing two more children. She did sometimes come with us when we were walked out in the afternoons by our nurse and always spent time with us after we had had our nursery tea and before collecting my father and then changing for dinner. The afternoon walks would be with the latest arrival in a big pram and with my parent's large Great Dane on a lead. The dog's name was Paulo and it had a sworn enemy nearby of the same breed and answering to the name of Paul. There was therefore some confusion when a fight developed, as it often did, and both names were being called by the respective owners with very little effect!

My chief recollection of these occasions was from the fact that, like most large dogs, ours was always slobber at one end and wagging tail at the other, and both were exactly at my head height. I have been perhaps over sensitive ever since to the predicament of small children whose inattentive parents fail to notice when a dog is applying unwelcome licks to their offspring.

With our older sisters, by six and seven years respectively, away at school, we younger ones were not expected by my grandmother to be too visible in the main body of the house during the day, although I do remember creeping down in my dressing gown to watch her in the early morning, impressive in her voluminous house coat and piled up hair, directing the cook, who had presumably come in early from somewhere in the village. I, as the oldest of the younger children and also, as I shall explain, effectively at the time the only male grandson, had, in addition to being permitted these early morning intrusions, certain treats during the day when my grandmother would summon me from the nursery and sit me on her knee in her drawing room so that she could read to me. The book I remember most, as no doubt a favourite of both hers and mine, was called 'Mr. Quill's Animal Shop'. In it the various occupants of cages in a pet shop occupied the dull time of early closing by telling, in turn, stories of their former lives and of the circumstances of their capture. Nearly seventy years later I tried the name on the internet and found that there was just one copy known to the web site and that it was at a book warehouse here in Barcombe, not two miles from where we live. Needless to say, I am now the proud possessor, for a fiver, of an excellent copy of my first remembered book.

At the end of the day, after we had been bathed and attired in our night wear, we were ushered by our nurse into the dining room to kiss the adults goodnight as they sat at dinner. We were then ushered out again, somewhat awestruck by the gleaming mahogany, silver and candles in an atmosphere far removed from that of our simply furnished nursery. To be fair to my parents, I am sure that my mother must have hated this existence, and indeed my eldest sister has confirmed that it nearly destroyed their marriage. It was probably less of a strain for my father. An artificial leg meant that he was restricted in his choice of weekend activities and the house at Balcombe did at least give him considerable scope in which to enjoy the gardening at which he became both skilled and knowledgeable. Some of our best times with him were when he returned from his London office on Saturday afternoons, when he would come to the nursery and entertain us with a fund of Belloc, Chesterton and such like poetry, which he knew by heart, accompanying the onomatopoeia with much bouncing of us up and down on his good leg. His Saturday suit was a reddish and very hairy tweed and the memory of it rasping my short trousered and sensitive skin is with me still. On Sundays he was very patient of our 'assistance' of his gardening and he was always a fund of information to any of us who were prepared to show an interest. One nursery visit was less of a success from our point of view, as he confiscated our favourite gramophone record of 'Teddy Bears' Picnic'. When I asked Iris why it had been taken away she answered, with an air of secret and superior knowledge, that the flip side, which our nurse had never played, at least not in our hearing, was for some extraordinary reason a song called 'When I met Connie in the Cornfield'.

My mother was the youngest of seven children, five of whom survived. She came from Teddington, where her father ran an insurance agency from the family home. She met our father when accompanying her elder sister to visit her fiancé in military hospital when my mother, anxious not to intrude, turned to speak with the man in the next bed, from which all else followed. Although I remember both my maternal grandparents they were, like my other grandmother with whom we lived, fairly old, and my mother's mother died when I was four. We were taken from time to time to visit my grandfather and my mother's oldest and unmarried sister, Aunt Nesta, who

*My grandmother, Catherine Clutton, with whom
we lived from 1933 to 1936.*

lived with him. They were both cared for by a marvellous family
retainer, who was also accorded the courtesy title of aunt and
who had been with the family for virtually the whole of her life.
She was rather ugly in her features, with much facial hair, but
she was wonderfully good hearted and I think it piqued my
rather authoritarian aunt that we probably let it show that we
younger children were more comfortable in the company of our
courtesy aunt than our real one. I used to dread going as I was
put in a small room somewhere on an upper floor of this tall
house where the only thing that I could see from my bed was a
picture of a be-whiskered and fierce gentleman glowering down
at me. I think my mother must have realized what was wrong

because on one visit the picture, much to my relief, had disappeared. The standard treat on these visits was for our aunt to put us all on the trolley bus that passed the door and to take us to Kew Gardens not far away. At that age I found the trolley bus rather more exciting than the Gardens.

It was said that my aunt had had an admirer in her youth but that every time he called my mother, the baby seventeen years her junior, would play up and Nesta would be told by her unthinking mother to go and do what was necessary. After several occasions of thus being left in the no doubt very straight laced presence of the generation that he had not come to see, the suitor apparently gave up the struggle. Poor Nesta! After my grandfather died in 1940 she continued in the Teddington house with the retainer, until she also died, running her father's insurance agency in neat longhand and supplementing her income by giving piano lessons until her death in 1971. She was an eccentric, getting about on an old bicycle until one day she collided with a pillar box. When asked how it happened she said that she had shut her eyes to offer up a short prayer for a happy day. She gave us all, other than my mother who was on tenderhooks at what she might say next, great amusement on her wartime visits by her uncompromisingly Victorian ways, by making no secret of her disapproval of my father's liking for a drink, and for insisting upon sitting bolt upright in bed reading with a tin hat firmly on her head.

My older sisters being largely absent during the week, we looked forward to their being at home at weekends and during school holidays. Iris and Shirley were good at organizing family games, such as rounders played on a triangular green formed by a road intersection just beyond the house. If there was traffic, and there must have been some, I don't remember it interfering with the game, or any dangerous moments when, as often happened, the ball was pursued across the road. They were also good at charades and party games and sessions of such things as Monopoly, which we younger ones were permitted to play with them so long as we did not upset the family pecking order by having the temerity actually to win. In fact, as far as I can recall, Shirley was always bank and, not surprisingly, she usually won!

My elder sisters used to fight a lot, trying to draw me in on one side or the other. On one such occasion when I was, I suppose, about five and they were rolling over and over in a fight on the floor I received conflicting instructions from the combatants, with dire threats should I succeed, or indeed fail, to carry them out. 'Pull her hair Rafe!' Shirley would command, in a rather unsporting way while locked in combat. 'Don't you dare,' would respond her older and, in her quiet way, much more formidable sister. So I adopted my usual stance in such situations and did nothing, relying on the fact that while Shirley could certainly be fierce, she was equally quick to forget all about it. My parents had some trouble with Shirley's temper and my father would occasionally administer mild retribution with a few taps from a gym shoe applied to her lower regions. On one such occasion Iris was told to fetch a gym shoe, when the whole thing was defused and my parents reduced to laughter by her returning with a spiked tennis shoe. In later life, and indeed no doubt for most of the time when they were young, my two elder sisters were quite close, but fierceness when young was certainly a characteristic of some of the female Cluttons. My father blamed the genes, no doubt with his two sisters and some of his aunts in mind, and was fond of telling the apocryphal story of one female baby having been born with teeth and corns; the former for gnashing and the latter from kicking.

My Balcombe grandmother had been very shocked by the elopement of her younger daughter and failed to communicate with her further, which was why she regarded me as her sole

The family in 1935. Back: Shirley (died 1986) and Iris, with Nigel;
Front: (L to R) Marigold, Rafe and Angela (died 1993).

grandson until Nigel arrived close to the end of her life. This
was a great pity as my aunt had a happy marriage and no less
than six sons who now contribute a large number of relatives to
the family total. My aunt's final tragedy was her death in
childbirth, when her infant daughter also died. My grandmother
used to give me little homilies based upon her perception of life
and of its fundamentals. I recall one such when I accompanied
her to the village butcher and she said 'We live in a changing
world Rafe but you can still rely on some things. Best quality
sirloin steak like this is twenty pence a pound (or whatever; I
can't recall the exact figure) and always will be.' She wore skirts
to her ankles, a velvet band round her neck and white hair piled
into a bun which I thought was part of her head. It was always
with a momentary shock, therefore, that I watched her donning
her hat, which she did for every outing even just into the
garden, where the last part of the operation was a brisk stab with

a long hat pin, apparently through the middle of her head. She
started each day, as I have said, in her housecoat organizing the
household routine, then spent much of her time seated in front
of her folding card table, with her smelling salts bottle close at
hand, playing what was known in the family as 'grandma's
patience'; better known, I believe, as Double Napoleon or Up
and Down King Street.

Occasionally I would incur her displeasure, as when I fired
my pop gun in her direction and the cork travelled all of
eighteen inches before dropping at the limit of its string. The
standard punishment for such enormities was to sit stock still on
a chair in a chilly hall until she felt that a lesson had been learnt;
a process that could sometimes absorb much of what seemed
like a very long afternoon. Almost my last recollection of my
grandmother of whom, despite her sternness, I must have been
very fond, was when we had gone on a family outing to the
London Zoo and had arrived home well after both our and her
bed time. We children were ushered up to her bedroom – my
first, and last, visit – to say goodnight, to be confronted with
what at first appeared to be almost a stranger; a nightgowned
figure with an uncharacteristically small head, sitting up against
a pillow and with long white hair flowing over her shoulders.

This must have been shortly before my parents decided that,
if their marriage was not to crack under the strain of the last
four years, they must again have their own establishment. One
near miss, thank goodness, was a farm house literally miles from
anywhere, which would have made logistics very difficult when
war came. As it was, the final choice, another former farm
house, was nearly a mile from the village centre at Ardingly, but
at least we had neighbours and, until the last quarter mile, a
reasonable access road. My father signed a twenty one year lease
with the Balcombe Estate that owned the farm and much of the
surrounding countryside and we moved, complete with Sybil

and our maid Nellie, as I have said, in late May 1936. My grandmother survived one more year, presumably cared for by the aunt who lived not far away. She had had enough of war and I am glad, looking back, that she did not see the next one. I still have the medal she was awarded for her auxiliary nursing during the first war. When my father was taken to a field hospital in Flanders and told that his leg would have to come off because of gangrene he, at the age of twenty and no doubt in a very bad state and barely conscious from this and from other severe wounds to his face, did not want to spend his life as a cripple, as he then saw it, and would not sign the consent form. The family story was that my grandmother was informed by telephone at her home in Kent and somehow managed to be conveyed across the Channel during the night, to arrive in the field hospital in the morning and to sign the consent just in time. Whether she would actually have been able to make such a wartime journey, or whether she gave her consent by telephone, I am now not sure, but either way, we all owe her quite a lot!

CHAPTER 2

Family Home

THE HOUSE to which we made what was, for us children and no doubt for our parents as well, a most exciting move was the last one in the dead end lane by which one reached it. Turning right round the unfenced duck pond, with open fields and distant views of the South Downs and the Balcombe railway viaduct to our left, we breasted the upward slope of the last fifty yards of the bumpy and cart wheel rutted lane, passing our new home on our right and having our first view of the post and rail fenced farm yard on the left that was to be our closest, and sometimes too close, neighbour. The front door of the house was directly opposite the farm yard, where there was no space for stopping without risking obstructing farm traffic, mainly in the shape of the horses being able to get to their stable. It was necessary therefore to drive past the front door and the farm yard and adjacent farm buildings until the road ended at a parking area to the north of the house, where there were a range of storage sheds, a separate garage and, usually, a large pile of cord wood logs for the fire. Consequently, other than when special efforts were made to lead important visitors to the front, the usual entrance to the house was via the back door and into the kitchen.

Although the approach impression was of a stone house under an old tiled roof, journey's end revealed a northern extension of brick with tile hanging. The older, stone, part had been the original farm house and was reputed to be four hundred years old, with a resident complement of suitably period ghosts. It consisted of a large living room extending right across the house from east to west with a second, smaller, room to the south that was to become our nursery, flanked by a staircase to the floor above. The northern extension added a dining room reached from one door from the living room while a second door gave access to the front hall, from which in turn were reached the kitchen and large adjacent dairy and a cloakroom. The hall was just large enough for a coats cupboard and the Great Dane's basket, so that anyone rash enough to ring the front door bell was greeted by the deep barking of the large dog that was just the other side of it.

A second staircase led out of the dining room to our parent's room above, with a bathroom over the kitchen to which our father hopped in the morning along the connecting landing; a time signal which meant that the rest of us must soon get up. This landing also led to a sort of dressing room, with no external wall and thus no window, and through this to a large bedroom almost the same size as the living room below. From the exit from this room one arrived back at the first staircase landing, with a bedroom to the south of the house, above the nursery, and with the corridor doubling back to a small bedroom and family bathroom over the hall area beneath. When we first arrived the younger of us had great fun running through the house up one staircase, down the other and round again, until the powers that be put a stop to it. The older part was very picturesque, with beams to the ceilings and wood sills to the door thresholds, originally to keep the rushes confined to the floors for which they were intended, and ledged and braced doors with oak latches. Floors downstairs were quarry tiled, stone or, in the kitchen, brick. Only the dining room had a suspended and boarded floor which, in consequence, was a step up from the living room. In the main room a huge fireplace occupied the wall between it and the nursery, wide enough for chimney seats at each side of the hearth, on which logs up to six feet or so in length were burnt on two large iron dogs. The chimney started at the full width of this opening, gradually reducing in width but still some eighteen inches square at the top, where the rain was kept out by a slate supported on four brick bats. One of the stone walls enclosing the fireplace contained an inbuilt salt cupboard and both sides were deeply grooved from the knife sharpening of the generations of farmers who had preceded us.

While attractive, such a house was far from convenient in some respects, mainly because the only route from the kitchen to the rest of the house was through the family living room; a feature about which our nurse and maid, whose living room was our nursery, used to complain with some asperity, but only of course in the seclusion of the nursery and with the common misconception that small children will not take on board or understand what their elders say in their company. If my parents were conscious of this problem there was not much that they could do about it and when the war came and Sybil and Nellie departed to war work the problem solved itself. Another disability, not apparent until our first winter, was the draught demanded by the living room fire! One door had to be always open or the room filled with smoke. This meant that our lives in winter were spent toasted in front and freezing behind, remedied in part by high backed sofas and regular use of thick sweaters. There was of course no central heating and the bedrooms could be freezing in winter. My sister Angela became particularly adept at dressing in bed, seldom emerging on colder days until fully clothed. My parents did have a double bar electric fire in their bedroom, which may have helped a bit, and there was a single bar one in the big central bedroom, which had hardly any effect at all, but otherwise, as I say, at times we froze!

Downstairs, the big fire in the living room seldom went right

Town House, seen from adjacent farmyard.

out in the winter and there was a certain amount of residual heat
in the morning, which some of us made use of for dressing
downstairs once we had had a quick wash. The coke boiler in
the kitchen also provided some warmth, as well as hot water, the
former supplemented by my mother lighting the gas oven and
leaving the door open while she prepared breakfast. These
however were the downsides. There were many pluses; one
being that while we could be cold in winter the thick stone walls
of the main house kept it tolerably cool in summer. Mainly, the
house was fun to live in, as well as having a uniqueness that our
parents loved to show to guests and which we all enjoyed. If
there were a few inconveniences, and by modern standards
indeed there were, we children, at least, did not notice them.
The main impression of this small boy at the time was that the
house boasted the unheard of luxury of having four lavatories!

By the time of our arrival the house had been occupied separately from the farm for a number of years. Two pairs of cottages had been built by the Balcombe Estate to house the farmer and some of the farm hands. Town House, as our home was named, was left with a little over two acres of garden to the south, east and north of the house itself, the latter section containing an old disused two storey, four roomed building known in the family as the barn. Soon after our arrival my father was able to lease a further area of about an acre in extent, with a grass tennis court, to give us some three acres overall, including a well stocked apple orchard. Prior to the war years my father created an extensive kitchen garden, in addition to laying out a rose garden and flower beds. The ability to grow much of our own food, both animal and vegetable, was to stand us in good stead when food rationing came in. When that time came we also imported a pig arc and, with the help of the village butcher, were able, by the rationing rules, to add half a pig twice a year to our meat ration; the butcher keeping the other halves towards the ration distribution. We cured our sides of bacon and ham by rubbing salt into them and then wrapping them in muslin and hanging them in the chimney. I can remember,with feeling, that there is nothing like a salt rubbing session to reveal any forgotten scratches on one's hands! One year a cow's tongue was overlooked and when eventually extracted from the chimney was as hard as a brick and had to be thrown away.

I do not recall exactly how, when we first arrived, sleeping was arranged for us all. My parents had their bedroom looking east over the main lawn and my brother, then only just a year old, probably slept in his cot in the adjacent dressing room, with all four of my sisters in the big central bedroom. I was in the small room alongside the second bathroom and Sybil and Nellie must have shared what later on became the guest bedroom. The death of my grandmother in 1937 gave my father funds that enabled him to make several alterations to improve things. One of these was to turn the former dairy into a spacious larder, complete with shelves and wine racks. The old oak shelves were taken out and the local builder used them in his joinery shop to construct a large and many compartmented sideboard. In his old age my father's favourite post when he had visitors was by this sideboard, happily dispensing drinks and enjoying conversation. Another improvement was to create an additional bedroom within the roof, to which there was access via a steep staircase that led to the attics. It was only possible to make a small room as there was a huge tie beam extending right across the attic at about knee height that held the roof together. Also, the two windows giving light had to be fitted each within the width between rafters. Nevertheless, the room was large enough to accommodate two wartime evacuees, as well as me, for the short time that they both remained with us.

The next achievement of my father, who worked very hard during his weekends, was to convert the barn by creating a garden workroom and store room on the lower level and making the first floor rooms habitable as a playroom and small sitting room. Most of this he did himself and I, for one, was delighted to have a room in which I could lay out my trains – then 'O' gauge and needing quite a bit of space – without having constantly to take them up again because someone else needed the floor clear. Later, when war threatened the possibility that the house might receive a bomb, he moved some emergency furnishings, etc., to the barn in case we might have to take temporary refuge there. Fortunately we did not, as there were no 'facilities' and only a well, with a hand pump on it, out at the back. A useful find in the garden was a dry well, into which one of our gardeners nearly fell as it had only a boarded cover, hidden and rotted by years of turf accumulation. When invasion threatened we lowered the family silver and other valuables into this hiding place until the threat was over.

My father enjoyed a brief, and probably his only, period with money to spare after my grandmother died. When our grandfather died in 1927 he left it to his wife to decide how, on her death, the estate should be divided between his children. He did not live to see the elopement of his younger daughter but the consequence of this was that my grandmother's will left the estate to her son and elder daughter only. My father and his sister agreed to pass a part of their shares to their younger sister but there was still a very useful inheritance to each of them and my father was able to satisfy, at last, his twin passions for gardens and for the sea by building two large, heated greenhouses for the former and by commissioning the building of a motor-sailing yacht. With food for his large family in mind he also had a pre-fabricated chicken battery built just beyond the greenhouses. The foundation supports were put in by the local builder and the chicken house was erected and operational over the course of a weekend. The builders of the greenhouses, who had been proceeding rather slowly, were probably a little surprised and perhaps chastened to return to work on a Monday morning to find that a building had gone up alongside literally overnight.

The boat was my father's pride and joy, but alas only for two sailing seasons before he handed it over to Air Sea Rescue for the war duration, when it was used to recover ditched pilots from the North Sea. By the time that he got it back after the war it was in such a battered condition, as well as being covered in several layers of battleship grey paint, that he could not afford to restore it and had to let it go. Following its launch from Jack Powles' yard at Wroxham on 2 July 1938 however he made extensive use of it, with office and other friends and with some of us aboard during school holidays and at weekends. His last trip was to rescue Iris from an au-pair job in Berlin only a week

or two before the war began when, after traversing the Kiel
Canal, he was able to take up to the minute photographs of
several German warships that the Admiralty subsequently used
for identification silhouettes. When his boat was boarded for
inspection by the German authorities they were shown an
empty camera in the saloon while one of his crew hid the loaded
one in the forward bilge. The German ships' lookouts were
further distracted from the risk of their spotting the active
camera, in use through a porthole, by another crew member
pretending to have difficulty with the ensign halliard, so that the
lookouts had to watch through their binoculars for the moment
of dipping so that they could respond as nautical courtesy
demanded. It was a great risk, but my father was not lacking
when it came to courage. He was desperately disappointed that,
without his boat, he could not take part in the Dunkirk
evacuations.

The sequence of the events of this last cruise, as recorded in
photograph albums, is interesting. The German battleships
Sharnhorst, *Gneisenau*, *Koln*, *Konigsberg* and *Leipzig* were all
photographed broadside on at their moorings in Kiel Bay on 18
August, followed by the *Nurnberg* and a training ship, the *Fuchs*,
on the following day off the south coast of Denmark. My father
and his crew, including Iris, then sailed via Copenhagen,
Malmo, Gothenburg and Kristiansand, to arrive at Aberdeen on
30 August, with the intention then of sailing home down the
North Sea. On 1 September the boat was aground on the sands
somewhere off the coast, no doubt from attempting a short cut,
which must have been somewhat frustrating in view of the radio
reports of the ultimatum to Germany! My father got as far as
Grimsby on 2 September and evidently decided that that was as
long as he could risk remaining at sea. He was, I know, at home
on Sunday the 3rd when the ultimatum expired and the war
started. He was not to see his beloved boat again until once

more in Grimsby after the war's end, when Shirley and I went with him in the summer holidays to bring it home to Shoreham; making vain attempts to scrape some of the grey paint off what should have been bright varnishwork on the way. Half way into the Wash for our first night's stop one engine failed and we were just able to crawl on half rudder into a berth by nightfall. And that was it!

My father was totally immune to sea sickness and smoked his pipe continually, as was his wont, even in the roughest of seas; a practice of which friends with delicate stomachs became a little wary after a while. After the war, when he no longer had a boat of his own, he would sign on as cook on a Fleetwood trawler in order to spend a holiday at sea. In view of our parents' gardening interests, one or other of our Christian names had a floral connection. In my case my second name was linked to 'Lillium Henryi', as my father informed me when I asked why I was the odd man out. When it came to his boat the chosen name was 'Naromis' made up from our various names. Thus, the 'ro' was from my parents, Robin and Rosalie, I and S were my elder sisters and A and M my younger ones, with my brother supplying the N and my own name doubling with my parents' initial. My mother's name was seldom used, other than by her sisters and those friends who did not feel that they knew her well enough to use the 'Aggie' by which my father always addressed her. This confused new acquaintances who would look puzzled and then ask me or one of the others whether her real name might be Agnes. The answer lay in our parents' bridge parties when they were first married when they and their friends took names from one of Stephen Leacock's books. My mother's was Agatha the Angular and it stuck.

My father employed two gardeners in those pre-war and briefly affluent days and we children were under strict instructions always to use the courtesy Mr when addressing or

Naromis *at Salcombe, August 1938.*

'Away Seaboat's Crew!'; Iris, Shirley, Rafe and friend.

German battle cruiser Gneisenau *photographed from* Naromis, *Kiel Bay, 19 August 1939.*

referring to the head gardener. The young under gardener came in for a lot of teasing from my sister Shirley, but he seemed to cope with this mild form of flirtation pretty well. Another, part time, gardener came with the garden extension. He seemed to me to be incredibly old – he was probably in fact about my current age, but with rather more in the whisker department– but he had great patience with an admiring small boy's company and questions and he earned my hero worship from his ability to pull up thistles and stinging nettles with his bare hands. He also showed me how to make rabbit snares with which to catch some of the multitudes that then over ran the fields and came into the garden.

When we first explored our new garden domain we were mystified by the fenced off exclusion of a small strip, for no apparent reason, adjacent to the farm boundary. This was explained late in our first summer when the strip was occupied one morning by a huge steam engine. This, we discovered, had to be in that exact position once each year to drive, with belts, the threshing, winnowing and straw baling machines lined up ahead of it in the particular positions and sequence whereby the corn shocks, that had previously been brought in from the fields, could be thrown down from a hatch high up in the barn wall to the man feeding them into the start of the production line. The dust was incredible but fortunately none of us children, whom the farmer allowed to mill around ostensibly 'helping', seemed to suffer any ill effects from it; not that the possibility was likely to have occurred to anyone at that time – any more than anyone appeared to consider the dangers of allowing children so close to largely unprotected machinery!

The farm was my playground, and later on that of my brother also, when I was not at school. At this period of my life, although I was part of a large family I was too young to be regarded as much of a companion by my elder sisters, and my younger ones were, naturally, rather closer to one another than to me, while my brother was too small to be a playfellow. I looked to the farm therefore for entertainment and to the few boys who lived nearby in the lane for companions. My parents, in the thinking of the thirties, were a little concerned at my choice of companions, but there was not much that they could do about it and I think they were amused at times to be able to call upon me to use my Sussex accent for the entertainment of guests. My circle of friends was enlarged before long by my joining the Church choir but at the outset there were two other boys of my age who, like me, came along to the farm to enliven their day. The Church choir paid twopence per attendance – two services and one practice per week – which equalled my weekly pocket money. Whereas however the pocket money went straight out on a comic and a few sweets, the Church only paid out about three times a year, so glorious moments came round when one was suddenly possessed of seven and six or so; a lot of money to a ten year old at the time.

The duck pond was our social centre and we spent many happy hours in it, with our shoes and socks deposited on the edge, engaged in naval manoeuvres with boats that we had made from bits of wood and a few nails. Contrary to my fears on the occasion of our first visit, the pond was no deeper than a foot or so, but it did have a lining of duck droppings that squelched between our toes as we moved around. This produced occasional outbreaks of boils on my knees but otherwise I don't think we bothered too much as we sought to defeat one another in our naval battles. I do remember though being quite happy to promise my mother that I would not attempt to swim in it! Even a small boy drew the line somewhere. When we were not sailing boats we went further afield, in fact over two fields, to fish in the nearest stream with home made fishing rods or, for smaller fry, with jam jars on strings. The fish hooks were acquired at a shop in the village that kept going by acting as parcels agent for the bus company and by selling sweets from large screw topped glass jars. With hindsight I sometimes wonder at how the shopkeeper survived but, small though his income must have been, he was adamant that he would not increase it by selling us fish hooks during the close season. On one such fishing trip we discovered some disused oil drums. Next time we went we took the necessary string and a few planks with which to build a raft of sorts, on to which we all climbed with our fishing rods; none of us being willing to limit the loading by standing back from this first voyage. Alas, the raft almost immediately became ensnared by tree roots and then quietly subsided beneath our combined weight, leaving us to wade ignominiously to firm ground.

The farming was at our doorstep and therefore a daily presence in our lives, audibly, visually and, at mucking out times in particular, by its assault upon our nostrils. The houses of the farmer and his staff were a safe distance from these farm side effects but my mother's kitchen was no more than thirty feet from the pig sties, with the stables almost as close. As well as the smells therefore the kitchen was seldom free of flies. Fly papers were the remedy for these and there were usually several pinned to the ceiling beams, with the unwary colliding not only with the sticky papers but with their complement of still kicking captives as well. My father would patrol the kitchen armed with a rolled newspaper, often when my mother was trying to cook. Fortunately he was in London during the weekdays and reasonable hygiene was preserved. My mother usually allocated one day in the week for her main cooking and baking, when she would look very professional attired in a white coat. She had a habit of storing everything in wrongly labelled containers, while always knowing herself where everything was. She would say 'Rafe dear, would you please fetch me the rice from the larder?

It is in the tin on the second shelf marked Demerara sugar' – or words to that effect.

The farmer suffered some embarrassment when cows were due for service as this was done in the farm yard where the cow could be brought from the stalls at one end while the bull, a ferocious and large Jersey that lived in a small enclosure at the other end, was led out by the farmer holding a pole with a snap hook through the ring in the animal's nose. Before doing this the farmer, a rather stern man of whom we were all a little in awe, would order any children that were nearby, and perversely we often were, to go back into our garden, from where we promptly took up station behind knot holes in the garden fence! Thus our education in these matters was fairly well advanced by the time that our ages reached double figures.

The farm gave a wonderful dimension to our early lives and the farm staff were very tolerant of children constantly watching their work and asking questions. Farming was quieter then and did not drown conversation. The farmer's son did use an early Fordson tractor but the farmer himself never used anything other than his two horses for power, trudging up and down fields for hours together behind a horse and a single, or at most two, furrow plough, according to the state of the soil. It was not long before I was permitted to help in a number of ways, including cycling to the village shop to buy their cigarettes as well as driving cattle, preparing animal feed and other odd jobs. I nursed a secret ambition to lead a horse down to the blacksmith in the village and to feel the pride of walking along the village street under the envious eyes of my friends while leading what in my imagination I hoped would be the larger of the two horses. Alas, I was evidently not to be trusted alone with such a valuable item of farm equipment.

The farmer and his son occupied one pair of cottages and the cowman lived in one half of the other pair, my father renting the fourth cottage for the motley succession of wartime gardeners that followed the original head gardener when he retired. The other hands were a pair of brothers who lived with their sister, all unmarried, in a cottage that could only be reached by walking across three fields. Their groceries were delivered by bicycle pannier as far as the cart shed, from where one of them carried them home. All of us collected our milk straight from the cooler in the dairy; seven pints a day in our case in two large jugs. Later, it had to go to some central collection point in churns and then come all the way back again before we could drink it!

My mother derived great amusement from the fact that three of the five farm staff were all called George but, by some minor difference of pronunciation in each case, there never seemed to be any doubt about which one was meant. To add to the confusion the daughter of the cowman, who kept house for him, and the sister of the two who lived across the fields shared the same name; both answering to Dolly. The cows and horses each had a name as did each of the fields that made up the farm. I don't recollect that the pigs were given the same distinction but there were quite a few names that one had to master before one could understand what everyone had under discussion. As I suppose was common before people became more mobile, in the village of Ardingly half a dozen surnames accounted for an appreciable part of the population. More by coincidence, the same thing applied in our bit of it. The farmer was George Parsons and our choir master and organist at the nearby parish church was another Parsons, who actually came from another village. For a time even the parson was named Parsons. He was a frequent and welcome supper guest, when he and my father, who was very well read, would settle down afterwards with the port decanter close at hand and have long discussions about theology and biblical interpretation.

A frequent attender at the farm was a man who had been part

of a large family brought up in another tiny cottage nearby that was also some way from any road connection. He was a little simple minded and no doubt incapable of holding a job and was thus the last of her family still living with his widowed mother. He was generally unshaven, apparently clad largely in cast-offs and went everywhere with an equally scruffy dog and leaning on, or waving energetically to assist his articulations, a gnarled old stick. He spoke in an indistinct and high pitched whine that was difficult to understand until you were used to it and his speech was punctuated by frequent sniffing. Despite his alarming appearance he was a kindly individual and he rather took to me as someone of about the same mental age. In response I thought him most interesting from the fact that he had three fingers missing from his left hand, which he proudly informed me had been taken off with one blow from a hedge swopping sickle. He was of even less help over farm tasks than we boys were but everyone tolerated him with good humour and on very hot days he had been known to divest himself of his jacket, still leaving a thick waistcoat, and actually handle a pitchfork. Mostly however he leaned on the nearest fence to watch the farming operations and was known in consequence as 'Old Weary'. In very hot weather the farm hands would remove their flat caps as well as their jackets, when the unaccustomed exposure of receding hairlines would reveal strips of white skin in odd contrast with their weather beaten faces.

When I see how much we all appear to need as the essentials of life today I often think of the simplicity of their lives, but also of the apparent contentment with which they lived the daily round and dealt with repetitive and often humdrum work. The farmer and his son had family lives and no doubt went a little further afield than the village from time to time, but the lives of the others were centred wholly on the farm. The oldest of them, who died shortly before the war started, told me that he had once been to Brighton, beyond the South Downs that he saw every day, and that he had also been a few times to Haywards Heath, the market town no more than five miles distant. Otherwise his life of some seventy years had been spent entirely within the village, no doubt farm labouring from the age of fourteen or earlier and with no thought of retirement. Holidays were spent leaning on the farmyard fence talking and watching, as a change to being in there working. While the newer cottages had electricity and water, the oldest had only oil lamps and a well. By the perversity of fate it was these with the least of modern conveniences that suffered the most from modern armaments a few years later when a stick of bombs fell right alongside them – fortunately with no deaths but with a good bit of shock!

Apart from the farm and pushing boats round the duck pond, the other enjoyment shared with my friends was the fishing already mentioned. In the summer, when we were not at school, this was done very early in the morning as we lived in mortal fear of the Balcombe Estate gamekeeper who was often in evidence later in the day. If we did but know, he probably had no interest in our activities other than amusement, but that did not stop us hiding our rods and running if we saw him in the distance; returning for them when the coast was clear. I would, on a good day, leave my fellow fishermen in the lane and enter the kitchen proudly bearing some small perch or roach which my long suffering mother would fry for my breakfast; no one else displaying much enthusiasm for them.

Life was not all fun and fishing of course. From Balcombe Angela and I had been sent on the bus to a kindergarten at Cuckfield but, soon after our move, I was passed to a prep school in Haywards Heath conveniently close, for fetching and carrying purposes, to the school attended by my older sisters. The prep school headmaster was an enthusiast of boxing and, as

I have always had a nose that erupts on the least excuse, I spent quite a lot of games periods well smeared in blood. Later, when I boarded for a year or so, I discovered that he also had an obsession with cold baths; not for himself of course but for the rest of us who were routed out of bed each day in order to stand in a naked and shivering queue, awaiting our turn for a supervised and near total immersion. He also decided that the quickest way in which to teach boys to swim was for them to jump in to the deep end of the school swimming pool that had recently been built, in part by the sweated labour of the inmates. In some cases it appeared to work but I let the side down by going straight to the bottom and waking to find someone leaning on my chest at the pool side and behind him a ring of anxious faces. Despite all this there were staff that we all liked and the school generally was a very happy period. It was a great disappointment to everyone therefore that it folded when the war came, in part I think because most of the staff joined up. Some boys went to the school nearby with which mine amalgamated but my parents decided to keep us at home as the threat of invasion loomed.

CHAPTER 3

War

A S HAS BEEN well recorded, the war started on a brilliant, late summer, Sunday morning. I can't have been in the Church choir on that morning as, when the – as it turned out, false – air raid alarm siren sounded at about midday I was playing with a boat by the duck pond. I heard my father calling me to come to the house immediately and I sensed an urgency in his voice that was almost my first realization that things were serious. Up until then I do not recall any feeling of alarm or concern at the prospect of war, no doubt because the adults had been at pains not to give children any reason to doubt the serenity of their lives. Over Sunday lunch that day my father cautioned us all, with a seriousness that for him was unusual in his relations with his children, that we must obey immediately and without question any call at any time to get under cover. We had had, of course, our gas mask drills at school and had been carrying them with us in their little cardboard boxes held by string round our necks for some time, but I remember little else that communicated to children any reason for which to be frightened. We were thus spared the very real worries that our parents must have had about the difficulties and dangers that lay ahead. At my level, almost my first experience of wartime restraint was to hear a lady customer in our village shop, where I had just emerged from having a haircut in a back room, complaining in no uncertain terms upon being told that her dog could not have his daily treat of chocolate because the shopkeeper had decided to conserve his stock pending rationing instructions.

My elder sisters both had bicycles and they became the proud wearers of arm bands that proclaimed their authority to carry important messages; from where to where or for whom I forget. Nor can I recall their ever having actually received a call to duty, but I at least was most envious of the fact that they were 'involved'. In fact, as the war progressed, it was astonishing how few people were left who did not have a uniform of some sort to wear on at least some occasions. My mother had her WVS uniform and my father first that of the Home Guard and then of an RNVR lieutenant. Iris and Shirley were soon in serving uniform and even I had my school corps khaki after 1942.

Important people appeared at our home from time to time to check on things like blackout precautions and contingency planning for the possibility of various emergencies. When however a bomb fell in a nearby field and failed to explode and the village policeman came in the evening to put into effect a plan to move us all to the village hall for the night, he received short shrift from my father, plus a doorstep lecture upon experience, or lack of it, of being under fire. We used to take it in turn to draw the blackout curtains around the house. This had to be done before lights could be turned on in the evening but, if one left it too late, it also had to be done in the half dark, which was no fun in an old and reputedly haunted house if you were of a nervous disposition, as I certainly was.

There were lighter sides to a state of war in those early days. One of the first things that happened was the removal of all road signs, so that if the Germans should land they would not be able to find their way about! How long the average villager would be able to deny knowledge of the direction to the nearest town when having a pistol held to his head does not appear to have entered the strategic thinking. As our lane looked to be the better route at its point of departure from the Ardingly to Balcombe road, this led to several surprised arrivals at our house including, on two occasions, substantial convoys of army vehicles which could only reverse direction by wheeling through a field until the tail of the column was able to leave the lane to allow the head to re-enter it. One of these occasions was on a Sunday morning when my hospitable father invited the commanding officer and a few others for a drink before resuming their journey, what time the heavy vehicles settled well into their wheel ruts in the wet field. The farmer cannot have been much amused and, soon after, the replacement of the 'No Through Road' sign at the end of the lane indicated that someone in authority had decided that such a concession would not imperil the defence of the Realm.

An excitement for me was the prospect of evacuees. The two who came to us were not genuine, nor were they complete strangers. One was the son of a distant cousin of my mother and the other was from a family with whom we were vaguely acquainted. I had been to visit the first at his London home and hoped to have a companion at last staying in the house but it did not work out like that. He was a year or two older than me and not interested in my, or indeed any, country pursuits and spent most of the time at a different school or with the local scouts that I had never wanted to join, having at that time, and indeed for most of my life, a disinclination for being in organized groups. Another problem was that our nurse Sybil, still with us in the early stages of the war, was inclined to make pointed and adverse comparisons between the virtues of visitors and the failings of the home team. This could be tiresome enough when children came for a party or for the day. It became very irksome, to me in particular as the eldest to whom it was applied, when it was a regular occurrence. For these reasons our first visitor, with whom I shared my bedroom and frequently my evening bath, became rather a disappointment. He stayed about a year before disappearing to a school in the West Country.

The second visitor was of very short duration. He was a year or so younger than me and had been, clearly, indulged since birth; certainly by our standards. To be dumped into our large family must have been a bit of a shock for him and I'm afraid he came in for a fair bit of ribbing. On at least two occasions my mother had to get the car out in a hurry when it was discovered that he had escaped, with suitcase, and she had to bring him back from where she found him on the London road! His mother arrived one weekend with a press reporter in tow, to take photographs of 'a typical evacuee in a typical country home'. Fortunately, my father was away or they would probably have been forcibly ejected. I still have the, heavily posed, photographs. An evacuee who came by the standard procedure to live with the farmer's son and his wife was much more acceptable and he joined the three of us 'duck ponders' in our fishing and other out of school pursuits, bringing to them an urban air of sophistication with which we were initially quite impressed until we learned to differentiate between what was genuine and what was embellished in order to impress the country bumpkins.

I don't remember exactly when my prep school closed. It was probably early in 1940 when the key staff left to join the fight. Our nurse and maid left soon afterwards in order to work in munitions factories and I remember my mother's mood of depression at finding herself without help and with a large home to run and family to feed. Most of us were allotted tasks to help out and daily helps of a sort soon arrived from the village, where my mother did a lot in a quiet way to help the less fortunate. One such task was to iron, on her electric roller iron, the sheets included in the washing by means of which a nearby widow lived. My father never discovered that one of his wife's daytime good works while he was in London was to take in the washing, or at least some of it, of a taker in of washing! Many ladies of the

My parents in wartime uniforms; WVS and RNVR.

village benefited, throughout the war, from the tea ration surplus generated by the combination of a large family and a preference for drinking it weak by those who drank it at all. My mother's distribution calls on her way back from the morning run to the station were keenly awaited.

I have said 'help of a sort' from the village because my mother's kind heart was unable to resist either suggestions for frequent and extended tea breaks or the giving of small parting gifts to her helpers when they left at the end of their morning labours. It got to the point that one such helper used to come armed with a holdall with which she seldom left without it containing the few tins, apples and the like that would be pressed upon her. There was however one bonus from the evacuation programme, as those sent out from London included a few adults. One of these was a most delightful elderly lady called Minnie who came to help my mother, complete with mob cap, a fund of East End sayings and an apparent ability to see spirits of the past in almost every room. She had lost her fiancé in 1914 and had never married. She was a rare 'treasure' and a great friend to us all.

Because my father was disabled and we lived five miles from the commuter railway station, as well as being nearly a mile from the bus stop, we had a small petrol ration that allowed the car, unlike the many that were laid up for the 'duration', to be kept running to allow my father to reach his work in London. Travel to school was more difficult, partly because the home journey would have meant an extra daily trip to which the petrol would not run. For this reason, and also because our parents were concerned for our safety away from home in the 'phoney war' period, my younger sisters and I, together with a few of our neighbours' children of similar age, were taught at home by my sister Iris, who had recently left school. This went on for about a year until other arrangements became possible and she left to join the WRNS, followed a little later by Shirley also leaving for the WAAF.

Those other arrangements in my case were a spell at the secondary school in East Grinstead, reached by a combination of a cycle ride, with several others from the village, to the Bluebell Line station at Horsted Keynes – then part of the Southern Railway's network – followed by a train trip and then walk through the town to the school. The trains had no corridors and covered the few miles between Horsted Keynes and East Grinstead fairly slowly. There was therefore quite a bit of communication between school passengers in different compartments by shouting from the windows, and not excluding going out of one door, along the outside and in through the next door, standing on the foot step and making use of some sort of hand hold kindly provided by the Southern Railway to these old carriages! The permanent way inspection staff used to collect the school caps thus blown off and deliver them to the Horsted Keynes station master. This forced the losers to report to his office in order to get them back; a request that he met only after first giving the applicant a stroke or two from a cane that he had acquired for the purpose. The down line at his station had a platform on each side, connected by a tunnel. The boys retaliated by watching as the train came in to see on which platform the station master, who was on his own and had therefore to be on the platform to clear the train for its onward journey, had placed himself in order to inspect the season tickets, then alighting by the other platform and escaping through the tunnel to the exit before he could check whether or not we had valid tickets for the ride.

The classes were co-educational and large, each with about fifteen girls on one side of the room and the same number of boys on the other. I was seated at the back, from where I was unable to read the blackboard, and felt largely ignored by teaching staff who seemed generally to concentrate on the nearer and brighter pupils at the front. I therefore learned very little and also, while my sister had no doubt done her best, that period too had hardly been one of top quality education. Consequently, when I sat alone in the headmaster's study in the summer of 1942 as the sole school candidate for the public schools common entrance examination I must have put up a pretty poor showing. By an odd coincidence, a year or so later I picked up a stray sheet of paper in a Tonbridge School corridor, to find that it was a page from my own exam papers. It was covered in the marker's critical red ink; no doubt typical of most of my submissions. Tonbridge, however, was under the bomber route to London and numbers, in consequence, were down to the low three hundreds. Exam results were therefore taken with a pinch of salt and almost anyone could be admitted. I was thus lucky and, with proper tuition for the first time for some three years, was able to rise through two scholastic years during my first calendar year and to join my better educated friends in their forms by year two.

That was still in the future. To return to the early war years, my allotted duties included caring for the hens in the battery house and the geese that were imported as lawn mowers when there was no longer petrol for the mechanical variety. This entailed a great deal of noise because ducks were running free range over the same territory and the drakes would take a fancy to the geese which the latter rebuffed loudly. Geese are dirty and inefficient lawn mowers, partly because they avoid the weeds. After a bit the lawns soon became hazardous for walking and unsightly from the clumps of nettles and the like that invaded them. Later on my father tried a pair of sheep, which were better and from which we harvested wool which my mother sent to somewhere in the Highlands where it was made into sweaters, but unbleached so that we all wore a striped and blotchy look when attired in them. A mistake was to hire a ram, which was supposed to do its work over the weekend and then depart but which was, following a heavy snowfall, not collected for a week or two, during which time it did a great deal of damage, including precipitating the final demise of the grass tennis court. I don't remember there being any lambs and in time the sheep suffered maggot attacks, from lack of proper dipping, and went the way of all flesh; in their case via the village butcher.

After all this I taught myself to use a scythe, which was certainly less trouble than the sheep had been and rather more effective, with the longer grass at least. Sixty years later I still use one; they are very good exercise. It must have been a great frustration to my father that he could not do these garden jobs himself. Wartime gardeners helped but they were generally a transient lot and often did more harm than good, like the one who announced to my mother over a morning cup of coffee that he had tidied up the 'asparier grass' by 'cutting down all them ferns'. When petrol again became available it fell generally to me to mow the lawns, cut the hedges and attend to other tasks that worried my father if they were neglected. The field hospital had made a less than perfect job of his amputation and he had varying degrees of pain for the rest of his life; so acute when pressure was low that he was sometimes unable to wear his leg in order to get to work. At home he wore the leg when any strangers were expected but otherwise often left it off to give himself relief, using crutches instead. On summer weekends he would be found from quite early in the morning, sitting on a sack and doing lower level weeding and pruning tasks with his crutches on the ground beside him.

The pig arc, put up one Christmas as surely one of the more unusual festive presents from a husband to his wife, accommodated one pig most of the time and sometimes two.

The open part of the enclosure was floored with disused railway sleepers and it never failed to astonish us how quickly a pig could root large holes in the creosote impregnated timber. The pigs required a great deal of feeding and my parents' friends, particularly those on the station car run, were persuaded to save swill which was collected whenever the car passed by. A great stroke of luck was the arrival of Canadian troops who were billeted in the disused old rectory adjacent to the Church at the beginning of our lane, supplemented by a barracks of Nissen huts. My parents quickly called on the camp commander, who rejoiced in the name Julius Caesar, firstly to offer Sunday afternoon tea to up to six or eight soldiers each weekend and, secondly, to ask to be allowed to collect swill. The soldiers were all raw recruits, many from the backwoods of Newfoundland, and self conscious from still having the shaven heads that were a first requirement upon enlisting as a guard against lice. The teas were popular, not least with my older sisters who saw few young males in our country isolation. First time visitors, who had been told by earlier ones of my guinea pigs, demanded on arrival to see the animal 'whose eyes fall out when you hold it up by its tail'.

Some of our Canadian visitors came from more educated backgrounds than others appeared to do. To these my father would offer the run of his bookcases; an offer that was taken up with alacrity by men situated as they were. I don't believe a single book went missing and every borrower was punctilious in returning them as promised. A spin off of this hospitality for me was that there was usually a soldier whom I had met in this way in the queue at the local cinema who could be persuaded to tell the ticket clerk that we were with him when we wanted to see a film to which children could only be admitted in the company of an adult. They would also let us in to the camp cinema, when we would be seated on the floor at the front to watch a rather distorted screen from a position immediately below it; all available seats having been taken by the troops who had little else to do in the evenings. On one occasion the film was the 'X' rated 'Cat and the Canary' and I recall a scary walk home in the dark afterwards. And in the country in wartime it was dark indeed, with no light from either houses or street lamps and little or no passing traffic, but with the advantage that there were sometimes wonderful night skies of an intensity that it is difficult for most of us to experience today.

The camp obliged with a regular delivery, by jeep, of almost more swill than we could handle and the smell of it boiling in a large container on the gas stove became, for a large part of the war, a feature of our kitchen and, when the wind was northerly, of much of the rest of the house as well. Much of what was thrown out had not been touched; some of it still in its original wrapping or container. Our hard pressed mother knew an opportunity when she saw one and our meat ration was often supplemented by what came in the jeep. This led to an embarrassing incident when the dog owned by a rather class conscious neighbour stole a string of sausages from a newly delivered consignment, which our neighbour promptly replaced from her household rations. My mother could not quite bring herself to admit to these people that we were in the habit of eating pig swill and that the dog had not actually done any harm. She therefore accepted the sausages with a good grace.

My recollections of life at home, during the early part of the war and before I went away to school in 1942, are of constant involvement with animals. Apart from those on the farm, a battery house full of chickens and the gaggles of geese, ducks and, for a while, sheep, we seldom had less than two dogs and a few cats and in the hutches I had rabbits, guinea pigs and at one time, until my parents drew the line, my two ferrets. To complete the picture, indoors were a bowl of goldfish and also various white mice; the latter only until they disappeared beneath the floor boards one day, never to be seen again. Most of this menagerie had been acquired at the Haywards Heath cattle market, with one or two errors along the way. For example, I had been under strict instructions to purchase only one guinea pig but the one that I brought home had already been got at and very soon, given the animals' ignorance of the laws against incest, I had nearly thirty of them. I was for ever building hutch extensions out of bits of wood and by raiding my father's stock of wire netting but there were frequent escapes, when one would have to chase the offenders through the tunnels they made in the long grass and return them to captivity. Eventually, one night the ferrets also escaped and by the morning my stock of guinea pigs was reduced to four. My mother had never liked the ferrets, partly because they often caught young rabbits in their burrows while their parents were able to bolt more humanely into the nets placed for their reception. I was also a little shaken by the guinea pig carnage, so back the ferrets went to the market. I was sorry to see them go as, among my friends, the ownership of a pair of hunting ferrets, plus a supply of nets for rabbit catching, had given us many an interesting and rewarding afternoon, with the full permission of the farmer, who was as glad of anything to reduce the rabbit population as our families were for the additions to the meat ration. My efforts to cure the skins by nailing them to the barn door and rubbing them with alum were less successful and family pressure soon forced me to throw the stinking pelts on to the bonfire.

My dog bitch, also acquired at the market, lived in one of the sheds and was regularly besieged by every suitor in the locality forming an expectant ring round her enclosure. Nobody seemed to get round to speying at that time, at least not down our lane, and we had frequent litters of some very assorted puppies, most of which were sold in the market, with the unsaleable residue asphyxiated by the local vet, along with the surplus farm cats. One Sunday a litter escaped and, during a quiet moment in the morning service, came bounding noisily into Church. Things were quite lively for a bit as we all chased them between the pews while the congregation looked on with some amusement. Eventually they were all captured and we were able to retire hastily and convey them home.

Not all such alarms and excursions were confined to the outdoors. My father was inclined to patent medicines and at one time took a teaspoon of wheat germ with his breakfast each morning from a tin kept on the dining room sideboard. One morning after this ritual I came in to search the sideboard saying 'Where are the goldfishes' ant's eggs? The tin was here somewhere.' This caused my father to rush upstairs (he could move quite fast when he had to) and to come back down again after a bit looking somewhat pale, while the rest of us seated round the table froze in anticipation of what might happen next. In fact all that happened was that the goldfish tank was banished to a window sill in another room and the ant's eggs were put into a new tin bearing no resemblance to that containing the wheat germ. This must have happened on a Sunday, when we breakfasted in state in the dining room and our mother would prepare a dish of kedgeree, or suchlike, as a Sunday treat. On every other day we had our breakfast in the kitchen, except my father who said that he had not been brought up to eat in the kitchen and to whom therefore our mother conveyed a tray to the dining room where he ate in solitary state. We were never quite sure how he would react to family indiscretions. At one Sunday breakfast, after I had read somewhere something that I had thought rather funny, I tried it on the family saying 'There was a good joke I read this morning. It was a news item saying "Father of ten shot, mistaken for a rabbit."' There was another

Wartime lawn mowers.

freeze. My mother appeared to have swallowed something the wrong way and as soon as I saw my elder sisters' faces, with looks as if they were trying to pretend they were not there, I realized that I had allowed my warped sense of humour to get the better of me. My father, as it happened, said nothing at all, for which I was greatly relieved.

Another animal alarm happened when uninvited fauna, in the shape of a rat, died under the floor of my parents' bedroom, forcing them to take refuge in the spare room while it fell to me to brave the stench, lift the floor boards and remove the corpse to decent burial elsewhere. But quite the most spectacular, and very short lived, visitor was a goat that my brother brought home from the market; I don't now know how, but probably in one of the farm cattle trucks that went there now and then. It was tethered to a post, with the idea that the post could be moved to provide fresh grazing, but either the post pulled out from the ground or the goat bit through its tether. Either way, the goat made a bee line for the young fruit trees and did more damage than anything had done before.

Apart from collection of pig swill, another extra-mural use of the family car was for what we called 'wooding'. This was a constant activity, incumbent upon all who took a walk in the fields, and by my mother stopping the car whenever she saw a fallen branch by the roadside. The reason was that, while our open fire seldom went right out during the winter months, the burning of four to six foot logs of diameter of six inches or more (the larger ones were first split with wedges) meant that large quantities of kindling were needed to get the fire going after an overnight lull; still more so if it went out. By the time the car was eventually driven into the market auction enclosure for sale, in about 1950, the family people-cum-swill-cum-firewood carrier was just about on its last legs and my father, in the front passenger seat on his way to and from the station, had on several occasions entertained onlookers by riding with his umbrella up because the sliding roof leaked.

I have said that the war did not impinge much upon us younger ones, but as time passed we all, of course, became more aware of it. Bombing raids and aeroplane dog fights were a familiar experience even in our country district and precautions at home included some of us bedding down under the dining room refectory table when raids were expected. Several bombs fell on the village, dumped by pilots who could not face the London barrage, and we looked with awe on the craters made in the woods by bombs and by crashed aircraft. My mother joined the WVS and my father the Home Guard, where he took some pride in being the only member of the village platoon, including a local architect who was the commanding officer, who knew how to strip and reassemble the machine gun with which they were issued. Home Guard meetings were in the village hall, or often in one of the three village pubs, where periodic training manoeuvres were usually designed to finish. For this service my father did not have to alter his appearance but when later he donned naval uniform he had either to remove his moustache or add a beard. He chose the latter, which had the advantage of covering the scars of the war wounds that had shattered his lower jaw and most of his teeth. I remember that it took us all quite a while to get used to his appearance when, at the war's end, he shaved it off again.

It was shortly after this time that, coinciding with my elder sisters having left for the forces and my departure to Tonbridge, my parents finally ran so short of money that they let the house for a year and took a vacant top floor flat in Oakley Street in Chelsea. My younger sisters were boarded with friends in Haywards Heath, while my brother became a boarder at his prep school. The various animals must have been sold. My parents, with their large family and the costs of education, had never been exactly over endowed with income but the situation had been made worse by the fact that my father worked for Schroders, then owned by its founding German family and with much business in that country, which could only survive the war by requiring all of its staff to accept a substantial pay cut. From her temporary London dwelling my mother applied for a job in a City office. At the interview the questioner looked somewhat disapproving when she said that her last work had been in 1919 and he asked her what she had been doing since then. 'Bringing up six children,' my mother replied with some asperity, whereupon an astonished employer took her on on the spot as his personal assistant.

This temporary removal from our home gave my father long enough to get himself commissioned in the RNVR, presumably partly on his record as an officer in the army in the first war as well as on his sailing experience. This commission enabled him somehow to beg or borrow an old naval vessel that was moored just below the Albert Bridge for use by a Sea Cadet group which he had formed, presumably with local and Admiralty encouragement and funding. Being the only member of the family with nowhere else to go, I spent my school holidays at this time at my parents' flat and well remember being enlisted as a sort of honorary Sea Cadet for Church parades on deck on Sunday mornings and for some energetic rowing of an old whaler on the river. A whaler is a heavy boat for young boys to power, particularly when against the current, but we all did our best under the interested eyes of Sunday strollers on the embankment who paused to watch the proceedings. This London interlude happened while the blitz was still a frequent night time occurrence and my mother and I used sometimes to sleep under the staircase while it was going on. My nearest approach to what my father would have called 'a shot fired in anger' came when a piece of shrapnel gouged a hole in the pavement only a foot or two from where I was walking through the blackout. I guess I jumped a little!

Having been too young to be of much practical use either in the garden or on the farm in our early years at Town House, by the time that the war was well under way, and certainly by the time of our return from Chelsea, we boys living in the lane were able to do rather more, especially during the summer holidays from school. During the long evenings of Double Summer Time every one of us who could do so worked in the fields until ten or so at night to get the harvest in. No one thought of payment; one was just glad to be making a contribution – any contribution – to the 'war effort' and in addition it was a lot of fun. In retrospect it always seemed to be glorious summer but there must have been wet days and I recall tedious hours picking from the corn stooks standing in the fields the ears that rain had caused to shoot. The farmer, one of the Georges, would hitch his two horses, Punch and Ginger, to one of the big wagons while his son would put the tractor on to the other one. Both would then be drawn down the hill to the fields, with their drags on one wheel to stop them coming on too fast, where we would all be waiting, armed with our 'prongs', ready to pitch the shocks up to the hand on the wagon whose task was to arrange them so that they would not fall off during the journey back to the barn. Prior to that stage, we boys were stationed round the field as the binders cut and tied the corn, working round and round towards the centre. As the island of uncut corn grew smaller the rabbits trapped within it would make a dash for the safety of the hedges and it was our job to catch them if we could. This was done by 'hollering' as loudly as one could while sprinting after the quarry, when the rabbit would often stop, confused, and one could pounce upon it and dispatch it with a quick punch to the back of its head.

Rabbits, as I have said, frequently supplemented our meat ration, or were sold in the weekly produce market in Haywards Heath with which my mother was involved, and to which our surplus chickens also went after I had killed and plucked them and my mother had drawn and trussed the carcasses. At one point one of the least effective of our temporary gardeners volunteered to do the killing, but he was so inept at it that on two occasions the poor birds woke up while being plucked, suspended by one leg and with most of their feathers removed! If, five years earlier, anyone had told my mother that she would be expert at drawing chickens she would not have believed them, but war forced a degree of self sufficiency and we were fortunate in being able to achieve this in our country home, including one Christmas lunch at which every significant part of what we ate came from our own resources. In the same vein, with every bit of suitable ground throughout the Country planted to produce food, if anyone had told us that one day farmers would be paid to keep their fields fallow, no one would have believed that such a crazy situation could ever come to pass.

My father was not normally to be found in the kitchen, other than for the occasional fly swatting foray, but he was a great enthusiast, with our mother, for preserving garden produce. They both spent hours in season bottling vegetables and soft fruit and pickling onions, in addition to making some very passable wine from ingredients such as rhubarb or dandelions; passable that is provided you avoided smelling it while drinking! We also spent many hours picking apples and then wrapping them individually in tissue papers before laying them on storage racks that my father had made for the purpose. We got through no more than half of them before, by Christmas or earlier, the rest had rotted. In time the racks rotted as well, after which the wrapped apples were put into barrels, but with not much more success. During the Autumn term at Tonbridge my mother would send me apples through the post, enclosed in used cornflake packets. I had not the heart to tell her that by the time that they arrived they were so bruised as to be barely eatable.

In our first year at Town House there had been a bountiful apple crop and my father, in a fit of enthusiasm, had a load of them sent to a cider maker. In due course two large barrels were placed in the dairy, as it then was, and guests were invited to imbibe. This turned out to be of mixed blessing to them as the alcohol content was very high and the cider could affect the knees. The son of a neighbour, who made little secret of his unrequited adoration of my sister Shirley, found after dinner that he could not rise from the table. 'We'll soon put you right,' said my father and left the room, to return soon after with a large bottle of castor oil and an equally large tablespoon, from which he forced the very uncomfortable suitor to swallow a substantial libation, what time the object of his affections spluttered with laughter from the other side of the table. My father, who was not particularly fond of cider, always swore that it owed its potency to the discovery of a dead rat at the bottom of the barrel. Be that as it may, we did not make cider again and my father turned his home brewing to the dandelion wine instead.

And so the day came for me to head to school at Tonbridge, kitted out I don't know how in times of clothes rationing with the minimum wardrobe that the school would accept. My boarding at prep school had been of short duration, so the experience was seen as a new one and our Rector took it upon himself to invite me to tea, presumably to prepare me for some moral jungle ahead. Poor man; it was so embarrassing that I have never forgotten it. He was quite old and would have been long retired but for the demands of war. He suffered lapses of memory in Church, as at evensong when he started a prayer for those lost in the sinking of the *Prince of Wales* and *Repulse*, but when it came to the point could not remember either battleship's name and had to be prompted in loud whispers from those of us near to him in the choir. The tea, just him and me, was followed by our both kneeling for his prayers. It was I'm afraid with a sigh of relief that I escaped to what I felt to be the lesser problems of a new school.

CHAPTER 4

School

ONE OF MY worries on entering Tonbridge School in
September 1942 was whether I would be able, unaided, to
handle the separate collars to my new shirts. It was in fact a great
and uncomfortable struggle for the first few days until, by
observation of those more sophisticated in these matters, I
discovered that the collar went outside the shirt neck band and
was not intended to straddle it. There were thirteen of us
forming the new intake into our boarding house, Hill Side. I
was not only the youngest but also the only one who had not
come straight from a prep school. All but two of us knew one or
more of the thirteen from their coming from the same schools
or from their families being friends and they paired off
accordingly for study sharing purposes. That left me with a total
stranger to share occupation of the last and meanest study on the
lowest level and least favoured study corridor. It was all a
bit depressing at first, although my study mate and I got on
well enough after a bit and indeed until he left the school
prematurely after three years, to go I know not where. He never
joined the Old Tonbridgian Society and thus became
untraceable but while he was with us he did achieve some
standing as a very effective wing three-quarter.

A dubious distinction on our first day in school was that I,
alone among those newly arrived in our boarding house, was
placed in the lowest school form. Here however I found another
Hill Sider who had arrived in the previous term and who
seemed to be glad to have a house companion. He turned out to

50

be a genuine 'thick' who, even at a time when the school was very short of boys, did not last long. He was nevertheless of a friendly disposition, as well as being rather large for his age, so that having him for a friend not only gave me someone with whom to share the ten minutes' walk back from the school to the house after work – the forms tending to come out at differing times – but also to see me generally through the first inevitably strange weeks.

Another piece of good fortune was my form master. He was one of several in the war years who were well past retiring age and who, but for the 'emergency' conditions, would have been replaced some years before. He was not only mellowed beyond the average but also relaxed in his dealings with his class and their education. No doubt he was well aware that he had been landed with the dubious intake, many of whom would gain little from too pressurized a teaching regime. While we were, of course, taught we were also treated to a fair bit of entertainment, such as his liking for reading Kipling's poetry aloud, accompanied by much banging on his desk top in time to the rhythm of the verse. Better still, when he heard my surname he immediately said 'Son of R J?' to which I answered 'Yes Sir'. From knowing nobody I was thus suddenly transported to the distinction of being recognized as a second generation scholar, my form master having been at the school long enough to remember my father whom he also taught. It wasn't much but it was better than having no connections at all in the areas of either prep school or earlier acquaintance.

Although it is now derided and largely, if not entirely, discontinued, the fagging system that then operated quickly fostered a spirit of friendship amongst the newcomers whereby we all got to know each other and combined, in a form of mutual defence as the lowest, for a term or two until relieved by the next arrivals, of the low. In fact, fagging was not the torture that those who have no experience of it make it out to be – at least, not in our case and in our house. Few, if any, of those entitled to use it abused it and the occasional errand running was taken in our stride. I was fortunate to be allocated as a personal fag, for duties such as study cleaning and the polishing of Corps uniform buttons and boots, of the school's leading classicist and a prominent, but also considerate, praeposter, as the term was used at this school. It was a sadness to everyone, and to me in particular, that within a year or two following a brilliant school career he died in a skiing accident. The trouble with the fagging system, for the fag that is, was that you were on call at any time other than when engaged in lessons, eating, prep or sleeping. A shout of 'boy' or 'kid', according to whether the summons was to the upper, study, or lower, changing rooms, corridor level, required one to drop everything and to run to the point of call, where it was usual for the last arrival to be selected for what ever chore the great man required. This often meant being interrupted in some leisure pursuit, such as listening on one's study radio to a favourite programme. On one memorable occasion the call precipitated the hasty break up of a study gathering for a game of strip pontoon; playing cards for money – not that we often had any – being strictly forbidden. This caused a more than usually frenzied rush as it was a requirement that the call must be answered reasonably attired.

New arrivals were put through a series of Sunday afternoon courses of instruction by a senior boy whereby we had to memorize such things as masters' nicknames, the list of school praes and other pieces of information governing the running and discipline of the School that were thought to be important. This process went by a derogatory name for paper and many a parent, anxiously awaiting a first letter from their son, must have been surprised to read that 'this afternoon we have been having a Bumph test'.

We felt a certain pride in our boarding house, as others no doubt did in theirs for differing reasons, because it was the furthest from the buildings where we attended our lessons and therefore was, in our view, also the most distinct from the school itself. It was one of the few boarding houses where from the start boys had both a study, albeit shared, and their own sleeping cubicle, as opposed to the open dormitories used elsewhere. In time, as the school and the houses returned to capacity, new arrivals were put into dormitories in my house also, but that was several years later. We also had our own small playing field where games could be played on summer evenings and on which, at other times, we could hone the rugby or cricket tactics of our house teams away from the prying eyes of our competitors. Above all, we had a house master, in the last five years of his fifteen years incumbency, who was liked throughout the school, where he was the senior chemistry master, and who was generally considered, via the comparative grape vine, to be most boys' house master of choice, had the choice been theirs, which of course it wasn't. Lastly, we also had a matron, an Irish widow with a strong brogue, who was greatly liked and respected by us all. We were thus fortunate in living in a happy ship; something that could not be said of all such houses.

We made our own cubicle beds, under the watchful checking of the Matron, and were required to put all of our clothes away and to leave the place in a tidy condition before departing after breakfast to school. Any failure in this respect incurred a fine of twopence per item not properly stowed. When I put on my jacket one morning I found a live mouse in one of the pockets. I knocked it on the head and left the corpse on the chest of drawers as a mild protest at the implied verminous state of the premises. The mouse was duly removed by someone during the day but the twopenny penalty for untidiness was still demanded in the evening on my return.

Soon after arrival, all newcomers were sent to the music school to have their suitability for the Chapel choir tested by the music master. I was commiserated with by my peers for being a fall guy, in their eyes, for having been selected. In fact I enjoyed singing and have felt ever afterwards that my subsequent modest contributions to amateur operatics and church hymn singing received some benefit from the five years of tuition that I had from membership of the school choir and choral society. To this day, a favourite resting place for my mind's eye is the decorated under side of the school chapel roof vaulting as seen gazing up at it from the back row of the choir stalls. It was a sad day therefore when, years later, the building was so badly damaged by fire. It has been rebuilt and restored magnificently and is no doubt much better in many respects but, for this ex-pupil at least, it can not wholly replace fond memories of the building as it was.

At this school, for almost the first time in my life, I received proper tuition and was able, in the classroom, both to see and to understand. In consequence I managed, as I have already mentioned, to pass through two academic years – the first one probably not too onerous – in the course of my first calendar year, and to join my friends in the same grades as them at the start of our second year. This was not without surprise in some quarters; particularly my French master who seemed mildly unbelieving to find that I had taken in rather more than he had thought possible from my performance in his set, in which I had somehow earned his early dislike. It is difficult now to recall much of the time spent being taught but one does remember how the innately gentlemanly and painstaking approach of most of the staff contrasted with the attitude of a few that were less admired. The hair puller, for example, who emphasized a point by grasping the hair, circulating your head until the eyes watered and then banging your forehead down on to the exercise book to drive the lesson home. Another, who infuriated me far more as I thought of how much my father was paying for the privilege of my sitting before him, would devote much of the lesson period to the enthusiastic picking of his nose.

These of course were the exceptions and, with hindsight, it has to be realized that many of those who taught us had stayed on for our and the school's benefit when they should have been comfortably retired. Most took great pains not only to teach well but to do it with friendliness, fairness and enthusiasm, whether in the classroom or on the rugby pitch, cricket field or river tow path. A few were frightened of losing control and showed it but were seldom exploited, although there were exceptions. A giant of a man showed himself to be terrified whenever the air raid siren sounded and we, by mimicking his terror, made things worse. For all one knows now he could well have been shell shocked in the first war, but we were not to know that and on several occasions we all, including him, crouched under our desks until it dawned on him that there was no actual danger. He also made the mistake of ordering anyone exhibiting a persistent cough to go outside and stand in the corridor. It was not until half the class were suddenly persistent coughers and absent that he realized that this was not such a good idea. Another, who was well past retirement and who had a reputation, whether justified or not I don't know, amongst the boys for elbow lifting, entered his classroom one afternoon to find all the light pendants swinging in one direction while the boys swung in the other. This was in addition to often finding a large chalk spider's web adorning his blackboard. His response, which in time we rather admired, was to wipe off the chalk with a cloth in an absent minded sort of way and to ignore completely any other manifestations as he proceeded with the lesson.

Service in the school Junior Training Corps or in the fledgling

ATC (the naval section was after my time) was compulsory and on one day each week we attended the first part of morning school in our uniforms, the last two periods following break being devoted to Corps training. In my first year the uniforms were still those of World War One and we were instructed by a venerable former RSM, with a voice that any town crier would envy, in the mysteries of winding puttees in such a way as, firstly, to ensure that they did not collapse round the ankles and, secondly, to achieve an equal interval to each turn of such width that the material did not run out before the breeches band was reached and safely covered. I can see now his beautifully waxed moustache and hear his uncanny ability to pick an individual from a parade of several hundred by a stentorian 'C company, rear platoon, middle rank, second man from the left; STAND STILL!' A sober moment on some of these parades came when we were all stood to attention as the commanding officer read out names of former pupils who had been reported killed in action. Before the war ended there were, more than once, the names of god-like seniors of my first terms.

We had a lot of fun on the Corps field days held in the summer term, when we were issued with blank ammunition for our old 303 rifles and felt very warlike as we scrambled through the wet bracken of somewhere like Ashdown Forest, stalking and trying to outflank others who constituted the 'enemy'. On one such outing drivers on what is now the main A26 road were surprised to find it closed by apparently armed troops, until someone realized that they were schoolboys and told the 'soldiers' in no uncertain terms to get lost. A less funny event was when a boy put a pencil down the rifle barrel on top of the blank cartridge, causing another to finish up in the sanatorium with a backside full of splinters.

The Corps was invited to take part in marches through the town on important occasions or in celebration of a wartime successes. We were formed up for these morale boosting exercises somewhere to the south of the railway station, together with contingents of nurses, civil defence, boy scouts, girl guides, or any other body that could muster a representative and uniformed group. We then marched proudly, to the beat of the school Corps drum and fife band, through the main street and back to the school parade ground, where the proceedings were concluded by some sort of address. The head boy of my house was the band major and spent many an hour on our house master's lawn practising twirling his mace, with derisory hoots from those of us watching when he dropped it. I ended my cadet career as a sergeant and rather fancied myself as a drill master. During my naval training others were sometimes allowed by our petty officer to drill us all, but he never asked me to have a go!

The school was run on well understood rules, with no concessions to the 'political correctness' of a later age, no consultation with parents at all so far as I was aware and not too much discussion with pupils either, other than to a modest degree with the senior dozen or so who constituted the School Praes as they were known. None of us thought this other than appropriate. In fact, I think we were all happy to know exactly where we were, even if we grumbled at times between ourselves or, as happened occasionally, attempted a protest. One such rebellion happened when the music master took it upon himself to write a new school song and then to impose it on the school in place of the time honoured old and familiar one. In some bush fire manner this caused outrage among the boys and culminated in large numbers, from most houses, obeying a call to assemble after evening prep in the street outside the music master's home, where we all sang the traditional school song lustily into the night air. Speedy use must have been made of the telephone because as we all returned to our houses the house masters were waiting. Ours was accompanied by an embarrassed head of house who, but for his office, would no doubt have preferred to have been with us. We were all lined up in a queue outside the house master's study to receive a few strokes each from his cane. The effect was pretty mild and I don't think that his heart was really in it, despite his attempt to appear outraged, but at school next day there were many walking gingerly as a result of their house masters having laid on with more zest. The music master was a good one, but without much visible sense of humour other than for hoary musical jokes. There must have been some plain talking in the masters' common room because, at the end of term muster, while we sang the new song, we sang the old one also, no doubt in the hope that honour would be satisfied while, at the same time, discipline would be seen to prevail.

The usual wielder of the cane was the head boy of the house, or occasionally his deputy. The house disciplinary code prescribed a system of 'cautions' for various offences and an accumulation of six of these led to punishment by the head of house in the boys' common room, with juniors obliged to turn up to watch pour encourager les autres. Despite the horror with which society now regards corporal punishment, and particularly the chastisement of boys by boys, these rare occasions hurt nobody very much, least of all the recipient who basked in glory among his peers for some days afterwards, with those especially privileged being invited to view the damage in the communal shower room. The penalty for not being present when one's name was reached at pre-breakfast call over was a half caution. A few enterprising sloths would calculate, towards the end of term, how many times they could safely enjoy another ten minutes in bed without incurring the ultimate penalty; the record slate being wiped clean at the end of each term.

I was normally much too law abiding to accumulate too many

cautions and in fact beatings were rare and usually applied to a few incorrigible evil doers. I was however among a number who decamped to a cinema in the town one Saturday afternoon to see *Henry the Fifth*, only to find on leaving the cinema that a master had been there as well who reported his findings to the head master. Cinema going was strictly forbidden for fear of all the diseases we might bring into the school from too close proximity to the people of the town; a risk that did not apply to masters apparently. In the eyes of authority however it was the defiance of the rules, rather than any risk of plague, that constituted the principal crime, and one of this nature, involving boys from several houses at once, merited caning by the headmaster, which was no joke. One was informed of this appointment several days before it was due, no doubt to concentrate the mind wonderfully as Dr Johnson would say. At the appointed hour, having queued for the honour outside, you stepped into a bare classroom, to be invited by the headmaster to bend over in the middle of the room, without the usual common room table on which to lean and by which to absorb some of the recoil so to speak that lesser offenders in the house enjoyed. For a serious and worthy man of middle stature, mainly known to the boys as having a fixation with the prophet Isaiah and for preaching over-long sermons in chapel, he could certainly show others a thing or two when wielding a cane! The only upside to this experience was that in the school tuck shop afterwards, the 'grubber' as it was called, several people took the quite unprecedented step of offering me a part of their sweet ration. The main lesson for life of all forms of school punishment was that, once over, all was forgotten and the slate was wiped clean, even at the highest level. One of the party on this occasion was in fact appointed as head boy of the school not much more than a year following this incident. Although we were naturally in some awe of this headmaster we only learned much later of all that he did to hold the school together in difficult wartime conditions and to enhance its reputation in the process.

Wartime conditions were something that the boys just accepted and at times found rather exciting. By the time that I arrived the Allies' fortunes were, of course, beginning to turn and we followed the course of events keenly, from newspapers that were put up on boards daily in one of the assembly rooms, where boys could read them during break or at other times. The threat of invasion had passed. That of occasional bombing remained but did not bother us very much. Although we were under instructions to get under cover during alerts, these instructions were not followed too closely and the occasional dog fight in the sky above us was far too interesting to miss, although I do remember running for shelter during one cricket match when pieces of shrapnel began to hit the pitch. Later on, Tonbridge was close to the line of the doodle bug runs to London, the first of which buzzed over on my fifteenth birthday. A large number of these were shot down around the town, or brought down by fighter pilots tipping them off course with their wings. During this time we often had to decamp at night from our beds to bunks set up in a brick air raid shelter in the garden, where the practice for a time was for someone to read by the light of a torch from a book of ghost stories that I, for one, found far more alarming than the enemy without.

During the day we had a grandstand view of some of the battles from the fire escape at the northern end of the house and were sometimes the first to see where a plane or buzz bomb had come down. School timetable permitting, boys were often first on the scene and there was a lively trade in exchange of various bits of metal and not a few cannon shells and other rounds of ammunition. Our house master must have got wind of this as we were lectured severely after prayers one evening on the dangers of picking up such things but, as he was far too nice a man ever to invade the boys' side of the house during the term, tuck boxes bulging with armaments remained undetected. When VE day finally came, the school was given a day's exeat and I cycled home, where my mother found me a bottle of beer with which to celebrate; the first time that I had been considered to be of so advanced an age as to merit such an offer. I hated the taste but would not have admitted it for anything.

Daily exercise was compulsory, unless matron ruled otherwise, and we had to write our compliance each day on cards displayed for that purpose. Often this would be a commitment to a team game of rugby or hockey in the winter or cricket, tennis or rowing in the summer. Boys with well heeled parents played games such as rackets or squash, while esoteric ones took to fives. On other days one could opt for a run, a kick about under supervision on the house field, or a spell in the gym. For a time in our house one compulsory afternoon each week had to be spent cultivating a large vegetable garden that had been cut out of part of the playing field in furtherance of the 'Dig for Victory' campaign. I enjoyed rugby but only reached the school third fifteen which, despite its modest attainments, had the distinction of being one of the heaviest teams on record. I still have a photograph and some of them were certainly beefy.

I did not enjoy cricket, partly because I was not very good at it and also because it took up the whole of an afternoon. After one year one could apply to join the boat club instead. This, if you were accepted as I was, had two advantages. One was that, because it was at some distance, it allowed a bicycle to be brought to school; a privilege otherwise limited to senior boys. The second was that the swimming pool was en route to the boat club, which gave one time to row and swim both in the same afternoon. We rowed in fixed seat fours; it being thought at that time that sliding seat fours or eights would not be able to

Tonbridge School Boat Club; First Four, Summer 1947.

cope with the bends in the Medway river. The school First Four, to which I was promoted for my last summer term, did well in general in its racing fixtures but the record was rather spoilt at the most important event of all, the Marlow regatta. An Old Tonbridgian with a home nearby invited us to a strawberry supper which on the following day rendered our stroke unable to do much more than swing to and fro in time with the rest of his crew. As I rowed at two I had to do my best to compensate and to avoid the cox having to do so by applying too much rudder and thereby slowing the boat. We managed to lose by no more than a canvass, the part of the boat ahead of the oarsmen. But for the strawberries we might have crowned the season with a spectacular victory. C'est la vie!

Another sporting disappointment was cross country running, or rather the lack of it, during our final spring term. I had been fortunate in earning my house colours by doing well in the school 'cras', as the annual main school running event was named, and our house had potentially a strong running team that included the school running captain for the year. But then we suffered the hardest winter for many a year and every running fixture was cancelled. The cold in both school and house was severe and staff and boys spent several weeks clad in overcoats. Regulations for closing schools when temperatures drop below a certain level were unknown but the coincidences of a fuel shortage and a flu epidemic must have constituted a nightmare for those in charge. As for us, we found comic relief in skating and tobogganing; the former on the flooded pits beside the railway from which gravel had been extracted to build the embankment. These pits were ideal for skating, if a little hazardous, because they were much longer than the average lake and one could get up quite a speed before having to turn round. The authorities had to deal with several injuries, plus a near drowning when one of our number fell through the ice.

Fortunately the weather warmed up in time for the sports day at the end of the term and my house had its annual photograph taken in the summer term with a record number of trophies displayed in front of the grinning boys. The final event at the end of the summer term was a concert performance, music only, of one of the Savoy operas in the main assembly hall. The masters and their wives hogged most of the principal parts and my nearest and only approach to the giddy heights of being a 'principal' was to be given the one line Mikado part of Pish Tush singing 'Why who are you who asks this question?' Prior to leaving from my last term I had obtained a provisional driving licence and was permitted the crowning joy, against which all else paled, of being allowed to drive the family car home, what time my mother sat in the front passenger seat nervously gripping the door handle and stamping on the floor with her braking foot.

It seems to be fashionable to decry one's school days but I enjoyed most of mine. I was fortunate in the friends that I made and in being able to present my parents, who I was well aware had made great sacrifices to send me there, with reasonable exam results, plus a few literary prizes. One of these was for writing a sonnet, which delighted my house master almost as much as the announcement, shortly after the war, that the Crown Jewels had spent the 'duration' in the prison at his home town of Shepton Mallet. He evidently had to endure a certain amount of common room banter about the lack of literary attainments among his scientists, of whom I was one, and my sonnet must have enabled him to counter the accusation. A final school accolade, of a sort, came towards the end of my last term when my house master called me to his study and asked whether I might stay longer as there was going to be a bit of a clear out at the top and I could well be appointed head of the school. It was tempting, but I had had enough and was anxious to move on. Also I knew what a burden the fees were to my father and that he still had to complete the education of my younger siblings. So I had to decline, but it was nice to be asked!

On a summer day, with exams completed and time to spare, a friend and I walked into the National Service registration office in Tonbridge and both asked to serve our compulsory two years in the Royal Marines. Our wishes were noted and in due course he was called to the Army and I to the Navy. So much for choice as we walked out into the long anticipated excitement of the post-education wide world.

CHAPTER 5

His Majesty's Service

My Naval career can hardly be described as glorious. Years later a retired admiral was appointed secretary of the Royal Institution of Chartered Surveyors. He was a man with a distinguished war record of responsibility for the protection of Atlantic convoys but in 1947 a lesser charge was that of coping with the National Service intake at the time of my involvement. He said to me 'We really did not know what to do with you all. Two years was too short a time in which both to provide adequate training and for the Navy to get some benefit from it afterwards.' The answer, for me and many like me, was to be used as dock labour, particularly for those tasks that unions would not allow their members to undertake because of the working conditions; but more of that later.

I was required to report, on 22 September 1947, to HMS *Royal Arthur*, a 'stone frigate' training establishment at Corsham in Wiltshire. My first encounter, on entering the gates and asking a passing uniformed sailor where I should report, was to receive a reply that was friendly enough but which assailed my unaccustomed ears with a masterly display of the 'f' word used as adjective, noun, verb or as required. Later of course, this became only too familiar, even if one strove to retain for oneself a more acceptable vocabulary; as many did; it was not universal.

My next recollection is of a sort of aptitude examination. We new recruits were seated at desks in a classroom and given test papers to complete. These were very simple and in part consisted of pictorial choices. You were confronted, for example, with drawings of a spanner, screw driver and hammer, each with an adjacent box, and an invitation to tick the box next to the picture of the tool you would use to tighten a nut. Strange to relate, but some questions really were that simple. In case the choice might be too difficult, as perhaps these papers were for the ten per cent of the intake that proved to be illiterate, a benevolent chief petty officer was at hand. He acted as a sort of roving invigilator, but one who stretched his role somewhat. I remember him leaning over my shoulder and offering assistance, on the lines of 'If I were you Sonny I should tick the spanner.'

This preliminary sifting lasted for about three weeks. During it we were kitted out with shapeless, working, 'square rig' (i.e., bell bottoms and jumper) uniforms, huge black boots, seamanship manual, 'housewife' for running clothing repairs, and so on and were given some preliminary square bashing, presumably to adapt the shapes of our feet to those of our inflexible boots. We were then transported to the next training stage at HMS *Raleigh* at Torpoint in Cornwall. This was another stone frigate – the hope of going to sea in an operational warship did not come to pass in my Navy – but on a much larger scale. We were allocated to dormitory huts, each with two long rows of double tier iron bunks, with a small stove in the middle of the hut to provide us all with warmth and comfort! I was assigned a lower bunk – as it happened, close to the stove, not that that made much difference – which was at least easy to get into but you had to watch your head when you sat up. It all made one's school sleeping cubicle seem, nostalgically, quite palatial. There were a few rough diamonds, including the first of such that I had seen with razor scars on his face, but also many good sorts, all finding the surroundings as strange as I did. I made some good friends whom I still remember well. Even the scarred individual, who was inclined to detect an insult in almost any utterance and whose remedy was to lash out, became a friend of sorts as I seemed to be able to calm him down on these occasions, for which some of the others were grateful!

It was at *Raleigh* that we were given medical tests, ostensibly to determine what class of rating our fitness, or lack of it, might dictate for each of us. It was on this occasion that the doctor, giving me a simple eye test, must either have taken one eye as representative of both or tested the same eye twice, thus failing, as I subsequently discovered, to detect that my poorer eye was not up to the standard necessary to the main, seaman, class. This, as it turned out, was fortuitous in shortening my time wasting service by some six months, but at the time it led to my being given a pair of standard, Naval issue, steel spectacles; hideous wire things with flat metal ear pieces to prevent poison gases entering a gas mask, because even my good eye needed some reading assistance. Another outcome of these tests was that I was the only one, in a hut of nearly fifty recruits, who did not have to go to the camp dentist for treatment. Some had never been to a dentist in their lives and there were a lot of drawn teeth in those first few days at *Raleigh*. Replacements were slow in coming, particularly it seemed for incisors, which someone in the hierarchy considered to be less essential or urgent than molars. One poor chap spent our time at this establishment with a hole in his face through which you could have posted a sugar cube, from having had all four central teeth removed.

We were paid once a fortnight, by means of a short formal parade designed to impress upon the recipient that he was lucky to get it, meagre though it was. However, there were compensations. The food was good, beer in the canteen very cheap and each man had a standard issue of two large tins of tobacco each month, suitable either for a pipe or for rolling into cigarettes, according to choice. I was not clever at rolling cigarettes and had already experimented with a pipe, of which my father, as a life long pipe smoker, approved so I opted for that, being regarded as slightly idiosyncratic as the only one of my acquaintances to do so. This wasted some of my tobacco allocation as our breaks for a smoke usually only lasted for the time it takes to burn through a thinly rolled cigarette, so that I was always knocking out a half smoked pipe. Not that a little waste mattered as the issue was more than enough for most of us and ingenious means were used to smuggle it 'ashore' where it could be used by friends or, more likely, sold. Some would march in agony through the barracks gate and then fall with relief into a shared taxi where they could remove their boots and transfer their contents to some more suitable container before we reached the station. The funniest incident that I saw happened on a very hot summer day at Chatham. We all piled into railway carriages for our weekend leave, when a sailor opposite me pulled off his hat, forgetting its contents, whereupon a pound or so of loose tobacco fell on to his open square rig collar and his perspiring skin, to which it stuck firmly.

The first thing that we all did as soon as we had accumulated a few fortnights' wages was to visit a naval tailor to be measured for a 'tiddly suit' and to buy a pair of deck slippers. The tailored uniforms were close fitting and an enormous improvement on Navy issue that were anything but and which nobody other than a new recruit without the option would wear outside of the barracks. It was a great day when, for the first time, one could at last walk out or go home feeling like a real sailor, rather than sneaking along in the shadows hoping people would not notice how raw and newly recruited one looked. Other presentational details also occupied our attention. One of these was to boil a Navy issue square rig collar until its blue/black colour gave way to one more reminiscent of the sky on a summer's day, although some old salts would deliberately wear unfaded collars, no doubt to distinguish themselves as genuine seamen uninfluenced by such trivia. Uniform change over from winter blue jersey to summer white, tee shirt style, 'vest' beneath one's uniform jumper happened by decree and did not always coincide with a change in the weather, so the tougher element (tough because the outer garment was scratchy to the skin) would cut a long sock down one side and suspend the top end, which looked much like the neck of a jersey, under their uniform jumper to avoid wearing the jersey itself. This was all right until a kindly duty officer one warm morning ordered the working party on deck to remove jumpers and then burst out laughing as several were left with nothing above the waist but a sock, tied round their necks with string.

The same thing could happen with the summer rig. Hardened salts with a dislike of washing clothes unnecessarily could buy white plastic dickies, complete with a blue band at the neck to resemble the uniform white shirt, which could be worn to look very much like the real thing. This however did not always fool the officer whose job it was to inspect leave takers to ensure that they were properly dressed before being allowed ashore. Detecting a dickie, he would hook his finger under the bottom of the vee of the collar and flick it out to stand in a horizontal position above the sailor's bare chest. This meant that the victim had to go and dress himself properly before presenting himself for reinspection, assuming the officer was still available, and in any case missing the trot boat and having to wait for the next one.

Training at *Raleigh* dealt with some of the basics, with instruction in knots and splices, firing a rifle and elementary aspects of working a ship at sea. Also, whether as a simple means of giving us exercise or whether the authorities really wanted us to know how to do it, we were sent down regularly to a jetty on the Tamar where we spent hours rowing cutters or whalers up and down the river under the helmsmanship and instruction of our petty officer. Having enjoyed rowing at school I quite looked forward to these sessions, but a heavy naval cutter is a very different proposition to a racing four, as I remembered from my father's Sea Cadet Corps, and it was hard work to get much way on the boat. These trips took us past rows of moored and decommissioned destroyers, corvettes and mine sweepers; ostensibly held in reserve but, in fact, never to go to sea again and destined only for the scrap yard. I had yet to discover that my service to the Nation was to consist entirely of adding to this expensive collection of scrap metal.

We spent a lot of time square bashing and after a while became quite good at formation marching. I still have photographs taken at what served as our passing out parade, when each trainee platoon was marched past a saluting base on one side of the enormous parade ground, complete with its huge mast and spars that were used to train some recruits in the arts of going aloft; but not us I'm glad to say as I don't think that my head for heights would have been up to it. During drill sessions one could often see, out of the corner of one's eye, some poor chap running around the perimeter of the parade ground in full kit under the watching eye of a petty officer supervising his spell of being 'under punishment'. The usual offences were being adrift – overstaying leave – or returning to barracks too much the worse for wear. The number thus punished was small, but often the victim could be a repeat performer, some people never learning how to know when they had had enough!

Once a week we were herded into the large camp cinema to hear an improving lecture. This was regarded by the older hands as a chance to catch up on sleep. Attempting to combat this, a chief petty officer would walk up and down each of the two gangway aisles, in no unobtrusive manner, trying to deal with those members seen to be failing to give their full attention to the speaker. I felt quite sorry for the well meaning people mad enough to be persuaded to speak to us on some no doubt worthwhile subject, only to have their efforts punctuated by loud commands to 'Give that man a shake' or 'You there, sixth man in, row K, wake up!' One of these petty officers, a little man much shorter than those he was trying to control, had the job on camp dance nights of walking round and round the perimeter of the dance floor telling sailors to get back off it if they did not have a partner to allow them to dance. Most of us were in this position as the imported 'talent' were not only in short supply but could spot at once those of us who were green trainees and not the more mature, and wealthier, sailors that they had come to find. The result was that, while we all went along for something to do, most of us spent the evening consoling ourselves at the bar and trying to spin out a pint of beer for as long as possible.

We were of course allowed to go ashore on most evenings and the boat across the Tamar river was free, but we usually spent the evening wandering rather pointlessly through the Plymouth town centre, such as it was after bomb damage, or strolling on the Hoe where we tried not to step on those who had found company and were entertaining them in a horizontal position. Some of this was quite an eye opener for a previously sheltered schoolboy. In the hut I proudly displayed a framed photograph of my girl friend of the time to show that, despite my onlooker role while at Torpoint – a role shared by the majority of my mess mates – I was not without success with the ladies, or at least one of them, when at home. This did something for my morale and that of others like me and we all dutifully admired each other's photographs. When some of the others came back from weekend leave spent with their ladies however, I did not confess that I had not shared that felicity due to the fact that mine was still at school, and a boarding school at that.

I can't remember exactly when we finished at *Raleigh* but it was probably shortly before Christmas, 1947. After the passing out parade we were issued with travel warrants and sent off to one of the main Naval divisional centres, Plymouth, Portsmouth, Chatham or Rosyth. My lot fell to Chatham, although I discovered some time afterwards that someone had made a mistake and that I should have been sent to Rosyth, which might have been a more interesting location, albeit further from home. Our new homes were corvettes moored in Short Reach in the Medway, just off the entrance to Chatham dockyard. We were issued with hammocks and blankets and left to discover how to sling this new form of sleeping accommodation before the lights went out, as well as mastering the tricky business of getting into them. The first common error was to haul one's self up into the hammock from one side only to drop to the deck on the other. The next problem, usual on the first night until it was discovered, was that your weight caused the hammock virtually to close over your head and make your shoulders feel as if they had been in a vice all night. The first task on day two was therefore to find a piece of wood that could be fitted behind the head and between the outer supporting cords, to hold the hammock open at that end. The next was to experiment with the tension of suspension to find the happy medium between being held in the vice like grip of too tight a slinging on the one hand and being so loosely slung that one woke in the morning having roughly the shape of a banana, if not with a crick in the back as well. Having got all that right, sleeping in a hammock could be quite comfortable and one got used, in a crowded mess deck, to having someone else's head or feet only an arm's length or less distant. Fortunately, our work teams were usually well below the numbers for which the ship's mess decks and hammock rails were designed, so that we were able to spread out; an advantage when there was so much smoking in bed.

We were soon disabused of any hopes that we might be sailors who actually went to sea. Our task was to 'mothball' the ships on which we lived, partly because it solved the Navy's problem of what to do with us and also because, as we soon found out, much of the working conditions were so disagreeable that Dockyard workers would not do it. The idea was to remove rust, inside and out, and then to preserve the ship in paint ready for storage against possible future recall to active service. Most technical equipment was removed and guns and other exposed armaments sealed, with their turrets enclosed in some sort of webbing which was also then painted. I started in a Corvette, HMS *Carron*, where most of the ship's company were national servicemen like me, with a few officers and petty officers to supervise the working teams and enough engineer and other more seasoned crew to keep the essentials of even a permanently moored ship working. We lived on the mess decks and we mustered on the upper deck each morning to be allotted various tasks. These were tolerable on deck or elsewhere on the superstructure, if tough on the hands, and the painting, later on, of the interior was similarly congenial enough. The less enjoyable tasks involved crawling into all sorts of narrow places and crevices where rust was suspected of lurking, the worst of these being in the double bottom to the hull. Our job was to enter through deck manholes to work between the inner and outer hulls; a distance of, I suppose, not more than three feet for the most part. At least, if the actual headroom was more than this, it certainly did not feel spacious to those of us working within it, particularly as, while the inner deck was level, the outer hull was not, so that working space diminished the further in one went. Armed with a pneumatic chipping lead in one hand and a wandering light lead in the other we had to crawl to the furthest extremity of each section, removing any rust that we could see as we edged back to the

Naval Service – Ashore and smartly dressed.

On board and rather less smart!
Cable greasing party, HMS Carron.

manhole, and then moving on to the next section to repeat the task.

Those in charge were then supposed to check that all rust had been removed but more often than not they took our word for it, being reluctant to get dirty. The next task was to use a suction lead to remove the rust thus loosened and then to go back in, still with the light lead but this time with a pot of red lead paint with which to paint so to speak the floor and the ceiling plus the vertical flanges that connected them. This was no easy task as part of it could only be done lying on your back and the sloping outer hull made it difficult sometimes to keep the paint pot upright. The last bit had to be done kneeling on the inner deck and sticking one's head, shoulders and painting arm in through the opening. The smell of paint in that confined space was almost overwhelming. This painting stage, we learnt, had to be done thoroughly as it was inspected, by torch through the manhole, once the paint was dry and if we had missed a bit we had to go back in again. Handkerchiefs were always red from the dust expelled from our lungs and noses and the Navy's remedy, no doubt on the advice of some expert who had not actually seen the conditions for himself, was that we had to drink a pint of milk a day to wash the lead from the system! When I read today, nearly sixty years later, of the dangers of lead based paints, let alone clouds of red lead dust in a very confined space, I can't avoid a wry smile. As for the absence of any protection of the ears from a pneumatic hammer at work on metal only a foot or so away, I can only suppose that nobody had thought of it. Fortunately in my case, there appears to be no lasting harm – at least so far, but what was that you just said?

Work on the superstructure could be numbingly cold. I was one of a minority that possessed and wore pyjamas, but others soon bought a pair when they saw the benefits of wearing the trousers under one's uniform when working aloft on cold steel in a winter wind. Later on, when the weather was warmer, two of us were given a short course in paint spraying, after which we had quite an enjoyable time spraying gallons of battleship grey on to the topsides of warships in the river, assisted by others on deck who moved our supporting cradles along as we worked. Other tasks included things like cable greasing – seemingly miles of it and very messy – turns of duty in the galley and, on one occasion, ammunitioning a ship. I can't think why this last was done as the ship was manifestly not going anywhere, least of all to fight anyone. This was my only claim to any sort of danger from my Naval service as I was detailed to bring on board a large box of detonators while everyone else, from the Skipper downwards, stood well back!

Recreation consisted of going ashore on the trot boat that went the rounds of the river reach, calling at each ship. My group of friends for these trips included one who was able to swallow a pint of beer in one go, without swallowing. This became known in a few of the Chatham dockside pubs and we sometimes benefited from a free round paid for by someone who wanted to see the trick performed. This could lead to quite a beer consumption in the course of an evening, we by this time being slightly better paid and having not much else on which to spend our money. I don't think we ever overdid it but others certainly did, particularly some of the older hands and on occasions an officer or two as well. In extreme cases, where a man was too far gone to climb the ladder from the boat's deck to that of the ship, those on duty had to swing out a torpedo hoist with a rope strop on it and thus haul the incapacitated individual up to be laid on deck for identification. I fear that some officers assigned to what must have been the very boring task of service on these ships did sometimes let the side down, but then we were all rather disappointed at the quality of our Naval service falling so far short of expectations.

After a time we were taken off these boats and transferred to the *Ausonia*, a former passenger ship moored in the inner of the three basins at Chatham. *Ausonia* had no engines, the space being taken up by fleet repair machinery. The story went that she had been so fitted as a fleet support ship for the invasion of Japan and had been towed across the oceans, via the Panama Canal, only to turn round and come all the way back again when Japan surrendered. I suppose the ship's company were, for the most part, still taken daily out to the mothballing tasks, but I was assigned to assist the leading hand in charge of the paint shop in the forecastle of the former liner. He knew a great deal about paint and its uses and I remember being shown tasks such as graining and producing various other surface effects, most of which I fear I have now forgotten. *Ausonia* was much more spacious than the *Carron* and the dockside facilities were directly accessible via the gangway. One of my friends was a barrow boy who taught me something of his skills at snooker in the seamen's mission, including a never to be forgotten evening when I potted all of the colours in sequence. Alas, that is another skill now largely forgotten. There were several older seamen on the mess decks, including many 'three badgers', indicating long service, who were waiting for discharge. Some of these had fascinating first hand stories of their wartime service and the dangers they had experienced but took in their stride. One that stuck particularly in my mind was being in the magazines, below the water line and behind watertight doors that would not be opened for any reason while the ship was in action. These men, whose job it was to put ammunition into the hoists that carried it to the guns, knew that if the ship were to be holed they would have no chance of getting out and would certainly be drowned. I felt a great respect for some of these old salts, men who would be the last to think that they would be entitled to be respected by anyone. They in turn thought that I

My parents, after a weeding session in the rose garden at Town House.

was little short of an Einstein as I finished their *Daily Mirror* crossword puzzles for them when they got stuck. A fair exchange I suppose, but I was sure that the balance of respect was to them.

Towards the end of my service I discovered that the Navy paid for tuition courses so I enrolled at the College of Estate Management, now part of the University of Reading, and started the correspondence courses leading to the first of the three main sets of examinations of the Royal Institution of Chartered Surveyors. My mess mates were impressed to see me sitting studying at the mess table of an evening, but whether by my industry or my madness I was not quite sure. One incident did however impress them. My Godmother died and I obtained a weekend pass and travel warrant to attend her funeral at Hastings. Many of my Naval friends had never heard of a Godmother and thought that I had ingeniously thought the whole thing up. One asked me whether I thought that, after a decent interval of a few weeks, he might try the same trick!

My Naval career came to a premature end when we all had to be put through a periodic medical test. The eye test was done by an efficient WRNS officer who was certainly not going to miss an eye or test the same one twice. Thus it was discovered – surprise, surprise – that the sight in my left eye was such as to disqualify me from the seaman class. My divisional officer called me in and explained that I would have to be either a stoker (engineering rating) or, perhaps more suitable in my case, a writer (clerical rating). He went on to explain however that once accepted into one rating class I could not be made to transfer against my will and that the alternative was to be discharged as unfit. I told him of my career intentions and that I was already studying for professional exams and that, if he thought it all right, I would prefer to be discharged so that I could get started on my next life. This was accepted and on a grey day in March I was lined up in the dockyard, complete with kit bag, with one man who had gone deaf and several who had flat feet. The Chief Petty Officer assigned to deal with us, doing a job that he evidently thought to be beneath him, informed us that, because we were unfit, we could not join the Royal Naval Reserve. Much we cared, we were to be free! On the command 'Right turn. Dismiss' we fell out and turned eagerly towards the dockyard gates for the last time. At times I felt that I had slightly let the family down; both my father and a brother in law having held Naval commissions, but, on reflection, I did not feel that the Navy had given us all much opportunity exactly to shine or to be ornaments to the Service!

CHAPTER 6

Office Boy

THE FAMILY surveying firm, Cluttons, had six partners in 1949, two of these being second cousins to me but twenty and more years my senior. The cousin with the same surname, Cecil known as Sam, had while I was still at school told my father that the firm needed a new Clutton generation to continue the family representation. My father was equally keen that I, and later on my brother, should reclaim what he regarded as the birthright denied to him by my grandfather having taken the capricious view that one could not have a surveyor with an artificial leg. My own preferences were not really consulted; not that I had any strong ones at the time, other than to find some means of supporting myself, as it was evident that my parents were still hard pressed to complete the education of my younger sisters and my brother and could not spare pocket money for me. For the same reason, the thought of university never crossed my mind. This I have later regretted when I have seen the friendships that others have made during higher education, not to mention the improvement of their minds. On the other hand, many other trainees were placed as I was and a degree was not then so necessary to a job in the professions. On the plus side, there were advantages to my start right at the bottom in that this gained me direct working experience of basic tasks that those coming in at a higher educational and salary level often miss.

My father bought me a quarterly season ticket to start me off and on the first Saturday following my Naval discharge I took the train to London in order to be sure of the route and journey time from Victoria Station to the firm's office in Great College Street, being in mortal fear of starting off on the wrong foot by being late on my first morning. The thought that the train might not run on time did not enter one's head in those well ordered days and I duly presented myself for my first day's work the following Monday, 4 April 1949, to start my surveying career.

In the event I immediately got off on several wrong feet! Normally at that time, all newcomers of my age were started as boys in the post room off the main entrance hall; usually for about three months during which time their duties of dealing with visitors and making frequent deliveries and collections of internal mail around the office were intended to assist them to find out who everyone was and, broadly, what they did. My cousin, no doubt from benevolent but misguided motives, decided to skip that stage; something that did not exactly earn me brownie points with colleagues of the same age who had not had such preferential treatment.

Sam's next kindness was far worse. From the time when the partners comprised my great grandfather and three of his sons the practice had grown up in the office of telling partners apart by use of their Christian names, plus a courtesy Mr – Mr John, Mr Ralph and so on – subsequently extended to members of the Trumper family who were also in the partnership. Partners who were not members of one or other of these two families also got the Mr courtesy, but applied to their surnames, or simply to their initials. Sam chose to walk me round the office on my first day introducing me, the most junior of the juniors, as Mr Rafe and I could see the 'Oh yes!' looks on the younger, and some not so young, faces as we continued this embarrassing progress. Thirdly, prior to my arrival, I had been provided with a desk and a chair that, although modest, were rather better than most new arrivals enjoyed. It was not until several months later that a fairly senior man visited my boss, with whom I sat, and said 'So that's where my chair has got to. I have been looking for it for ages.' My apologies were accepted and the chair returned; my boss assuring the rightful owner that I had not been responsible for its abduction. And lastly, instead of being put in the large room used by the other juniors in my department, I was seated in the room of the department head, ostensibly so that he could train me and so that I could act as his PA, a task for which I was wholly unqualified.

Fortunately for me, the department head, Sydney Baker, was a man who had risen from the bottom himself and was rather more perceptive than my cousin. He introduced me to the others of his team by my unadorned Christian name and in terms that stressed my complete greenness and willingness to learn. As to greenness, to give me something to do on my first day I was told to go to see a man in the drawing office. He was preparing a lease plan of a vacant bomb site in the City of London and asked me to go to see whether or not the adjacent pavement had any pavement lights as if there were any it was the convention to indicate their presence on the plan. Having only ever visited the City to see my father in his office I first had to find the site. Having done so I saw that there were no 'lights' and reported back accordingly. It was some time before I learned that a pavement light was not a street lamp and I sometimes wondered whether that particular lease plan was ever contested.

I think the word soon got round that I was in no way out of the ordinary and I learnt a lot from my junior colleagues as to how the basics of the office worked. There was certainly no special treatment in my salary of £200 a year, which was lower than that of anyone else in the department. Again, I owed this doubtful distinction to my cousin who, as I discovered many years afterwards when looking through old salary lists, had started at the same wage. He evidently thought that what was good enough for him at age nineteen, twenty years earlier, was good enough for me. Six weeks after I arrived the son of the then senior partner, Peter Trumper, who was to become the leader of the agricultural business while I led the urban one, started at three times my salary. He was four years older than me and had the benefit of time at Agricultural College but in terms of surveying experience was just as green. His salary was probably nearer to the correct mark than mine was but Baker, who got to hear of this and told me, clearly thought that a greater attempt at starting equivalence between the firm's two leading families should have been made. Someone else's salary did not really bother me at the time, as it apparently did some who knew more of the firm's politics than I then did, of which more anon. Baker, who was one of those who saw further than I then could, said 'Never mind, the job that you are doing is far more useful than his', which I suppose it was at the time as it was more difficult initially to find something useful on the rural side that a brand new recruit could actually do.

It was the frugal reward that, after a while, forced me to take a room in Chelsea, through the introduction of my sister Iris who was working in Westminster as an assistant housing manager and had had it some time before, as this was cheaper than the cost of the railway season ticket plus the daily garaging at Haywards Heath station of the small motor bike that my mother had bought for me from the gardener to make my commuting journey a little easier. To begin with, however, I used the train, usually standing in the corridor as it was frequently full by the time it reached Haywards Heath from the coast. My then girl friend joined me for the home run, to which I quite looked forward as if a seat were found she would sit on my knee and if there were no seats we were usually jammed pretty close together in the corridor; a cosy end to the working day.

The work of my department was estate management of

5 Great College Street, Westminster. Cluttons' head office from 1904 to 1988. Photograph by Niall Clutton.

properties of the Commissioners for Crown Lands, as they were then called, mainly in the West End and by the river at Millbank. At that time the major parts of these Estates were let on ground lease and management functions were limited in practice to collection of the quarterly rents and occasional checks to ensure that lessees were complying with their repairing and insuring obligations. Treating such freehold estates as investments that needed to be worked upon to achieve their maximum potential was largely unappreciated at that time and emphasis was more upon dealing with war damage situations and the likely consequences of the new Town and Country Planning legislation. The work of the Crown urban management team, of which I was the newest member, was therefore mainly to do with the buildings that were not let on long lease but were 'in possession'. This term did not imply vacant possession, although there were for one reason or another always a few such waiting to be repaired and or relet, but was, and still is, to denote buildings where the freeholder is the direct landlord of the occupiers, without any intervening head leaseholder, with therefore obligations to repair, insure and provide other services. These, in multi-occupational buildings, would include the running of central heating and lifts and provision and supervision of caretakers, cleaners and other maintenance contractors, as well as ensuring that tenants complied with their lease covenants.

A more interesting side of management work was letting or reletting. Rent reviews were still in the future. The team included Baker's two senior assistants, usually two building surveyors, two secretaries and about three trainees like me. The three senior surveyors would often take one or other of the juniors with them when they had to make inspections for various purposes, including the granting or renewal of leases, all of which was interesting as one gradually came to understand what the work of such a surveyor involved. Otherwise, my main time was taken up with the chores. These included visiting caretakers to ensure that services were working as they should and checking all accounts before payment, including reading gas and electricity meters which were usually in the darkest recesses of basements where one had to search for them with a torch. We did not trust the authorities to read their own meters correctly in those days!

My level of assistant was the main contact with the staff that we employed on the client's behalf; the caretakers, lift men, boiler stokers and cleaners. From time to time they would receive a visit from someone higher up in the department, one of Baker's two deputies, but usually it was left to the juniors to check, by frequent visits, that everyone was working as they should, as well as being present when safety and maintenance inspections by specialist contractors were made of boilers and lifts. Some of these men were characters. We had a caretaker who lived in mortal fear of what he called the 'Westminister City Council', expecting that any day 'they' would descend on him with some frightful accusation concerning the building for which he felt himself personally responsible. Another was a diminutive lift man who was bald but who managed to grow about a dozen hairs on one side of his head long enough to be stuck firmly to his pate and to join up with the sparse growth on the other side. They were never seen to be out of place and I was tempted to wait outside on windy days to see what happened when he emerged. I don't remember many women cleaners because they had usually done their work and gone by office opening time, but I do recall Baker being amused one day to receive a note from one of them saying 'I am writing, Sir, to apologise for Mrs So and So not having come to work today. She had a baby yesterday and is very lax in these matters.'

A most pressing task in my first winter was to find fuel for the heating boilers of the buildings in our charge. There was a terrible fuel shortage and I spent hours on the telephone to the suppliers pleading for coke deliveries and then rushing out to the buildings in question to check with the boiler men how long supplies would last and whether temporary shut downs were necessary so that I could then call on individual tenants to keep them informed. It was a nightmare time but one in which the situation was understood, as long as you could convince people that everything possible was being done. We were all, agents and tenants alike, inured to having to work in our overcoats from time to time. Sometimes there were more enjoyable tasks, such as attending when demolitions of war damaged structures took place, as they still did at that time. Some of the most spectacular were former terraces, where the bombs had destroyed the houses but left the more robust party walls standing. They came down in a very satisfying manner. We used a contractor who traded with the name 'Knock 'em down Bill'. He was reputed to be illiterate but he certainly knew how to make out an account, or to ensure that someone did it for him.

Repairs had to be done in small doses, as and when building licences could be obtained and materials found. Our two department building surveyors were very different. One was working his way up the qualification ladder and was used as required mainly on the more up market parts of the estate. The other was older and, like my boss, unqualified but rich in experience; a funny little man with a perpetual cigarette and a dreadful cough who loped along as if his shoes were too tight, rather after the fashion of Groucho Marx, and who was employed mainly on the Millbank Estate; then in our charge and in a very run down post-war condition. He was Baker's brother in law and I think a slight embarrassment, but as a practical building surveyor at the minor and making do repairs level he was superb and I learned a great deal from him and from the jobbing contractors that we employed. This, largely residential,

Millbank Estate was nearly all in possession and that was where a lot of the building work had to be done. My first solo job was to make a repairing inventory of all of the street and front area railings on the Estate, which for some reason had not been removed for munitions making; probably from fear that people would fall into the front areas during the blackout. They were in a pretty bad state and my job was to record each defect, missing part or area of significant rust, railing by railing. It was a hot summer and I was pacing the pavements all day for two or three weeks, to the point that one day my blistered feet were bleeding into my overheated shoes. There were a lot of railings on that Estate!

During that first year or so the rent for my digs was just under half my princely wage but we juniors were kept alive by an excellent office canteen where one good meal each weekday was available for about two shillings. That did not leave much over but when I could not get home to Sussex I found that the theatre 'gods' could give one a good Saturday evening out for two and sixpence and for exercise, other than walking everywhere, the rowing boats on the Serpentine could take care of a Sunday afternoon quite cheaply. After about six months I think my boss found it possible to persuade the firm to increase my salary and it went up to £275, thus allowing me a little more breathing space. My landlady used to deposit rice puddings on the stairs outside my room and when times were very bad I ate them, but otherwise they were discreetly flushed into the plumbing. She could not cook like my mother! Once she knocked on the door and ventured in, probably to say that the bath was free as two or three sessions a week were included in the rent. I happened to be working at correspondence course papers in which she professed an interest but was slightly taken aback when what she saw was a quarter scale sectional drawing of a lavatory pan and its drain connection. She must have formed a rather narrow view of my intended profession from that one view of the work. She had two sons living in the house, one of whom was a taxing master and the only person I have ever heard of who, when his working suit became shiny, had a tailor take it apart and reassemble it the other way round. It was so extraordinary that it stuck in the mind.

Right from my first months in the office there were times when I was expected to be in the partners' camp and I found this dubious privilege difficult, not only from the risk that it could be taken amiss by the people with whom I worked but also because, in one aspect at least, I could not afford it! Clients being shown round the office by a partner, as happened from time to time, were led into the room that, by then, I shared with the other juniors in the team. I was introduced, but not the others! It must also have been apparent to my friends that I was sometimes asked to accompany Sam on his visits to the Clients when they never were. To their credit, I think they rather expected a little of this, but to me it was embarrassing; not least financially as I had initially only one suit that had been my Sunday Chapel wear at Tonbridge. As soon as possible therefore I had to buy a second suit in order to appear reasonably turned out on days when I had been warned in advance that I was to accompany Sam on such a visit. It cost me a whole £6 at the Fifty Shilling Tailors and I probably skipped a few meals in consequence.

In my first winter at work I was invited to be one of the firm's guests at the annual dinner of the RICS, it being assumed without thinking, I suppose, that I would have no difficulty in being suitably attired. In the event, my mother was more perceptive than my employers and somehow found the wherewithal to enable me to go again to Sir Henry Price's emporium, this time to purchase a dinner jacket. When I turned up at Grosvenor House for the dinner I discovered that

everyone else at the table, and indeed almost everyone in the
room, were resplendent in white ties. Fortunately, my dress was
considered to be good enough for a youngster and shortly
afterwards our neighbour at Ardingly offered me her late
husband's evening tails which fitted me very well and which I
still have, although now never have occasion to wear, almost a
century after they were first made. The late Harry Watney, who
became a Consultant upon the take over of his small City firm
in 1960, was a character and a raconteur, with some off the cuff
remarks that would stick in the memory. One of these was the
somewhat derogatory description of one of his employees as 'A
sort of clerk, Old Boy; the kind of chap who wears the same suit
two days running.' I knew the type only too well from early
personal experience! Ever since, when dressing in the morning,
I found myself thinking 'Did I wear this suit yesterday?'

A group of us used to meet in the canteen each lunchtime
but, to my embarrassment, Sam decided to show that he was 'of
the people' by joining our table. This not only cramped the
conversation somewhat, because the others were almost as
junior as I was, but my cousin bolted his food, seemingly
oblivious to its temperature. He was on to the second course
and then coffee while we were still dealing in a leisurely fashion
with what came first. He then gave us all the sort of look that
implied that we were a pretty time wasting lot and then left, as
he did everything, in a hurry. This at least enabled us to sigh
with relief and get back to animated conversation. Being both a
character – something that he cultivated carefully – and wearing
a habitual air of impatient irascibility, Sam could get away with
most things in the office. He got cross with people queuing for
the canteen to open for lunch, as he thought prematurely, and
thus wasting the firm's time. His remedy one day was to go up
and say 'You are all much too early. I am going to reverse the
queue', which he then proceeded to do, much to the shame of

one or two formidable ladies who were, I'm afraid, usually at the front. Years later when there was a power shortage, people were astonished to see the senior partner going round the office personally confiscating any electric fires that he could find!

I was sometimes invited to supper by a man who lived a few doors away in the square into which my street led. He had four daughters and was trying to find them male company. I am afraid I ate some good dinners under false pretences as by that time I had a new girl friend whom I had met in the office. It did not last long but for a while she made my otherwise lonely London weekends much more fun and I remember her, as I do all those who for however short a time paid me the compliment of enjoying my company, with gratitude. On one occasion I took her to Teddington to see my Aunt Nesta for a Saturday afternoon outing. We were whisked off to Kew Gardens where my aunt led us round in the authoritative manner that I remembered from childhood, drawing our attention to objects of interest. At one point she said 'Follow me, there is something particularly interesting through these shrubs.' There was too, in the shape of a couple on the grass who were rapidly approaching that for which the botanical gardens were not intended; not for the animal kingdom at least. It was the only occasion that I can remember seeing my formidable aunt abashed as she beat a hasty retreat.

During the latter part of 1951 the partners must have decided that I needed wider training and I was sent to Drivers Jonas to replace an assistant who was leaving to do his National Service. The senior partner, William Bishop, had been a senior manager at Cluttons and kindly took me on but no one told me that Cluttons were still paying my salary. I only found this out, to my embarrassment, when I was called in to William's office to be offered my first ever bonus and told that this came from my current employer and not from my previous one. He seemed as surprised as I was. By this time I was living at home again as, following my twenty first birthday, I had been able to collect a legacy left to me by my Godmother. I had a small income from the investments and I used the cash element to buy a proper motorbike which made me much more mobile, until I crashed it one morning against one of the street bollards in front of Buckingham Palace, luckily with little harm to me but with quite a lot to my transport.

Drivers Jonas was then a smaller firm than it is now, with a wider client base and more varied work than I had experienced at Cluttons. Also, the assistants, while attached to one partner for their main work, would be asked to assist others without the intermediate manager level that, for the staff organization of Cluttons' extensive managements, separated the junior assistants from much direct contact with the partners. While my main task was to assist a partner with the management of two client estates in Mayfair, I was also given a variety of experience working with others on various professional tasks as they came in. These included such things as my first house auctions, at one of which the partner auctioneer dealt in a masterly and instructive manner with the fact that there was not a single bid from the room, taking bids from the walls until he reached the reserve and then announcing that the prices bid had not been enough, so that the property was withdrawn. One would-be purchaser was canny enough to see through all this and having discovered, by this performance, the price level that was likely to be accepted, then signed the contract before we returned to London; a good day for learning something new! Another day out was with a land agency partner who seemed keen to show a youngster that he was still in his prime. One demonstration of this was his attempt to vault a barbed wire fence, whereby he slit his trousers, but what really made it a day to remember was when he swung a quarter girth tape round a large tree in order to show me how it

Sydney Baker, my first 'boss' and most respected and excellent tutor.

was done. The leather tape has a large ring at one end through which the graduated end is drawn to indicate the girth of the tree. He swung the tape with gusto and the ring hit him on the ear, whereupon he danced for a bit while I tried hard not to splutter.

The most interesting assignment was the appointment of the firm to agree, on behalf of the Coal Board, the compensation to be paid to former colliery owners in South Wales for all their above ground buildings. Most of these were houses and because the number was so large, tables of capitalization rates, percentage deductions for repairs, etc. were agreed in advance. Our task was then to determine by inspection into which category each building, or terrace of similar houses, should fall for application of these pre-agreed valuation multipliers of the rent. The rental schedules were supplied and there was not much room for argument as to the rental levels as these were all controlled by statute. Some were actually below the statutory levels permitted but the Coal Board managers did not dare proposing increases as to do so would risk the unions calling a strike. We handled this task by a partner and assistant driving down to Wales for about one week in three, leaving the intervening two weeks to keep the rest of one's work going and to do the calculations resulting from the inspections.

We stayed at one of two hotels, depending upon whether we were working in the western or eastern valleys. The Coal Board's western property management was based at Neath and our hotel was a comfortable one on the Gower Coast. In the east someone had found a former Country Club not far from the Board's office at Cardiff. When people asked us where we were staying we could not for some time understand why our reply produced some odd looks until we were enlightened by being told that the establishment had the reputation of being where businessmen from Cardiff took their fancy ladies at the weekends. If they did we saw no sign of it and it is all now a long time ago!

It was not possible or necessary to inspect every house since those in a terrace of twenty or more would be, for practical purposes, identical. The property managers who accompanied us would therefore pick samples, including in their opinion the best and the worst, for our inspection. Many of these houses were very comfortable and the tenants would find a key with which to unlock a front room containing the best furniture, probably handed down the generations and smelling strongly of polish. There were of course some bad ones, where one had to walk through quickly, take a deep breath in the back yard and then hurry through again to the street. On one memorable occasion we were warned that the occupiers wore very little when at home and, sure enough, we walked into the kitchen to find a huge woman standing at the sink with her back to us, wearing nothing but an apron that failed to meet round her by several inches. A house that stuck in my mind was some way up a steep mountainside. Its kitchen and bathroom were cantilevered over a stream, with water being drawn up to the kitchen in the upstream room and everything else being discharged back into the stream from the down stream chamber. I did not have time to enquire whether there were houses with similar arrangements either further up or lower down! Life on these trips was seldom dull and my lasting legacy from them is a reasonable ability to pronounce Welsh place names!

Nor was life managing Mayfair property entirely dull either. We had to go out on the Estate before the Street Offences Act had cleared the ladies and it was a common experience to have their wares shouted at one. One of my colleagues used to stop to negotiate, saying he had changed his mind when he thought he had driven the price down to its lowest level. On two occasions I knocked innocently at the door of a house I was due to inspect, only to have it opened by ladies telling me to come back in half an hour when they would be happy to oblige. One of these, a few years later and in Spitalfields, was accompanied by a dishevelled man who backed her up by saying 'Give us a chance mate and take your place in the queue.' On the higher plane, of talking to tenants to maintain contact and to ensure that the building management was working to their satisfaction, one of those whom I had to visit was Syrie Maugham, the some time wife of W. Somerset. She always seemed to be in bed, although whether from old age or laziness I was not able to determine. I was ushered into a large and poorly lit bedroom where I had to sit on the end of her bed while she talked. It was nothing to do with the block of flats in which she lived, but she was an interesting raconteur and I mention it as an example of the kind of thing that fell to a junior member of a management team. My partners managing large residential estates in Kensington spent quite a bit of their time on similar social visits. It was an essential element to the maintenance of good landlord and tenant relations.

It was on this Estate, bordering the southern end of Park Lane, that I had one of my early opportunities, as I thought it, to do something really effective. I was required to make regular inspections of the progress of building of a block of flats on the Client's land, in the course of which I noted the use of an unusual type of brick in the building of a load bearing wall in the basement. Hastening back to consult with the firm's building surveyor partner, he confirmed that the brick did not have the necessary crushing strength for the situation in which it was being used. He then supported me in an interview with the clerk of works and in getting what by then had become quite a bit of masonry demolished and rebuilt with the proper materials. As a relative junior I felt rather pleased with myself, as it was rare to find such a mistake and most of these monitoring inspections were, consequently, rather uneventful. Alas, it was all to no purpose as no sooner was the block finished than it was pulled down again to make way for the Hilton Hotel!

By this time, following the incident with my motorbike and the ages it took to have it repaired, I had my own car, an old Singer Beetle that I had bought off the brother of one of my workmates. One of my jobs was to inspect building progress by attending consultant's site meetings at industrial developments in Kent that were being funded by one of the firm's clients. I used this car to get there and, as instructed by the firm's cashier, submitted my mileage sheets for reimbursement of the appropriate sum. I discovered later that the senior partner was rather cross about this as the rate was the same irrespective of the make of car and he thought that, in my old banger, I was doing rather well at the expense of the firm. In fact, the clients usually paid these expenses and were not concerned as to the make of the car concerned. Also, I simply followed the rules; I did not make them. I used to drive my shabby old car to his house on a Sunday afternoon and then drive him in his very grand limousine to our Welsh destination; my car being shut in his garage where it would not disgrace his smart home by anyone seeing it. It was usually dark by the time that we returned at the end of the week and I would climb back into my car and drive several miles in a state of near blindness from the contrast of the lights of the two vehicles.

The car was notorious in several respects. It had a wooden body structure that was riddled with woodworm and wood floor boards between which my overcoat slipped one day, wrapping itself round the differential so tightly that, after the car had come to a sudden halt in the middle of the highway, I had to crawl underneath and cut it to bits with my pen knife. On another occasion both front mudguards, which were connected by a length of wire across the radiator, fell off simultaneously on to a main road in Hastings when the wire broke. The final straw came when the final drive, constructed of a stout pad into which two halves of the shaft bolted to give flexibility, ceased to function when the pad disintegrated, leaving the engine running, the gear engaged, but the car not going anywhere and a fearful banging from underneath. Happy days, when there was much less traffic on the roads and no one had thought of MOTs!

There was a lot more fun in working for this firm, both because one could be young and moderately care free, or rather leave it to those more senior to take the responsibilities, and because I did not labour under the eponymous label that could be a burden to a junior employee. In 1953 it was thought to be time to bring me back to Cluttons, partly because the main client, the Church Commissioners, had given serious thought to a proposal by their secretariat that all management of their urban estates should be brought in house. This proposal was rejected, but only after the then President of the RICS, by the drafting of a superb memorandum, had been brought in to persuade the Commissioners of the advantages of continuing to use external specialist and market connected firms. In the aftermath of this temporary crisis the partners wanted to show that they were not unmindful of the need to bring forward the next generation which, in what was still seen to be a family firm, meant producing another Clutton. Shortly before that point my employer had been kind enough to ask me whether I would like to stay with his firm and become, in due course, a partner in it. Perhaps it was wrong of him to do so in view of the arrangement that had been made with my cousin but, as with my house master in my last term at Tonbridge, it was nice to be asked!

CHAPTER 7

Wedding Bells

NOW STARTED, in the Autumn of 1953, my mainstream involvement with the family firm that was to continue, uninterrupted, until 1994. To begin with, of course, my role was still that of a relatively inexperienced, barely qualified, surveying assistant, so that the work was not so onerous that it precluded escape to other interests at closing time. In early 1951 I had become involved, I cannot now remember how, with a drama group in Burgess Hill and I acted in two plays with them before the leader of the group and his wife, two retired school teachers, became founder members of an amateur operatic society also in Burgess Hill and I joined in, acting the part of the Sergeant of Police in the first production of the new company, *The Pirates of Penzance*, later that year. Someone in one of these groups introduced me to twin brothers living near the town and it became our habit, with one or two others, to meet up on Saturday nights in the local pubs where, regarding ourselves to be confirmed bachelors with no time for the trivialities of girl friends – we didn't have any – we put the world to rights over many a pint, puffing on our pipes meanwhile with the best expertise we could manage. They were good friends and it was a much looked forward to weekly event at a time of my life that would otherwise have been a bit empty of social pursuits. Meeting up with friends at the weekends was not easy when living where we did and one could not garden all of the time!

At the end of 1952 we performed the *Yeomen of the Guard*, where one of the cast urged me to join the Weald Theatre

Group in Haywards Heath, firstly because it was more accessible of an evening to a commuter arriving home via the town railway station and secondly because the Group was, as I soon discovered, capable of putting on and directing some superb quality shows, including an annual New Year pantomime. As it turned out, little did my friend know what a service he was doing me! I was duly given the role of King Rat in the January 1953 pantomime *Puss in Boots*. It involved only a few short stage appearances and I spent most of the time in the communal dressing room, to the amusement of my new friends, sitting in my rat suit, less the head, swotting for my final RICS exams which were to be taken in April. The cast included a Principal Boy played by a talented, charming and beautiful girl named Jill who was known to me, but not closely, from having been at kindergarten school with my younger sisters and attending children's parties at our home. I knew her as one of the younger circle in the town but assumed that she was on a committed and unapproachable plane. In the pantomime she was one of the stars while I had a minor supporting role, so I knew my place and concentrated upon my exam revision.

Despite this lowly start I seemed to meet with the approval of the producer, who was also the pivotal lead performer, a comic genius and a very good stage director. I was given rather more rewarding roles in the Revue that the Group staged to celebrate the Coronation in the summer; an idea that was so successful that, unlike the pantomimes that ran for a week, we somehow kept it up for a whole fortnight. This enabled me to get to know Jill better, but I still assumed that she was spoken for elsewhere, as I was also but to a declining degree. At that time the meeting points for our young circle in Haywards Heath, apart from Young Conservative meetings and Golf Club dances, were coffee shops on Saturday mornings and, in summer, the swimming pool of the only hotel in town that had one; open to

The first production of the Burgess Hill Operatic Society, The Pirates of Penzance, on a very small stage!

the public for a small charge. With our Guardian Angels no doubt working hard behind the scenes, it was here that a group of four of us met by chance one afternoon and decided to continue on to the local cinema in the evening. As the other two were an assumed 'item', that implied that Jill and I were teamed up for the evening; one that we all enjoyed and agreed to repeat. Thus 'from little acorns, etcetera'.

Back at the office and to my estate management work, when I returned from Drivers Jonas the senior urban partner, Kenneth Marr-Johnson, another second cousin, asked me to sit as PA with the team manager responsible for the largely commercial, as opposed to residential, estates of the Church Commissioners in the City of London and the adjoining inner areas, particularly Finsbury. I don't know how he explained my presence to the man concerned, but what he said to me was 'I would like you to sit with Mr So and So and find out what he does all day', Kenneth himself being much too reserved a man actually to examine his managers personally and to ask them how they went about the work for which he bore ultimate responsibility. He would occasionally go on estate visits with his department heads and he signed all formal reports to clients, but by the time that I worked under him he was in his early fifties and had either forgotten, or perhaps had never really needed to know, how his managers went about their day to day work. He was a highly respected partner, but rather austere and held in a certain amount of awe by the staff. He had grown up, so to speak, during an era in which all day to day urban estate management was left to mainly professionally qualified senior staff and their departments of assistants. It really was the case therefore that, while his responsibilities to clients were very extensive, he had little involvement in the work, other than in major cases or on investment policy advice or the relevance of new legislation.

In fact my new boss, whom his assistants knew as Charlie, but not to his face, was a kindly and knowledgeable man, if a little lazy at times and not very well organized. Sitting close by in a not overlarge office and inevitably hearing one half of all his telephone conversations, it did not take me long to realize that he had a complicated domestic life, with a home at Broadstairs, a weekend retreat at Saltdean and some sort of weekday home in south London, from where he drove in each day to the office. How he did it on the sort of salary that the firm paid I can't think. Because of these commitments, he usually had an appointment out on one of the estates on a Friday afternoon, from which he did not return, and often a similar one on Monday mornings before he came in. He also lived in some awe of my cousin and took enormous pains over the drafting of reports that the partner would be reading and signing. One of these was several foolscap pages in length and he finally, after much retyping by his secretary, got it into form for presentation. It came back later unsigned and with 'split infinitive' scrawled across one of the centre pages. In the days before word processors, having to retype was no joke and I had to explain to a boss who was almost in tears what the term meant. He was a qualified chartered surveyor and therefore received the monthly 'journal', an octavo sized publication in a blue cover and with a brown addressed label stuck round its middle which had to be slit open before the contents could be read. He had an open bookcase with one shelf full of these journals, not one of which had had its wrapper removed!

Most of the work of a general practice surveyor is value related and knowledge of what values are comes from constant experience of one's own and others' work in the market place and the analysis of transactions to determine their basic ingredients such as rental and capital values per unit of measurement and the investment yields that relate the two. It was soon evident to me that the flow of, or indeed interest in, such information was fairly rudimentary. The attitude of some of the firm's lifelong managers was that the firm was so well established and large that it supplied its own information bank, which to a degree was true except that there was no central means of making the information accessible and few bothered too much to enquire into the results of a colleague's work. An example of this attitude was that when I accompanied Charlie to fix the rent to be paid for a warehouse he told me what he had agreed in other cases. I then pointed to a 'to let' board on a property over the road to ask what rent was being quoted, to be told that that property was not on the Estate so he didn't know.

It was by instances such as this that one of my early impressions of Cluttons was of a need for a much more enquiring and commercial approach to our urban management work. Charlie's other assistant, who subsequently became my lead assistant and then partner for work for the Church Commissioners, had the same view that I did and in our work involving agreement of rents and prices we started to enquire of other firms for information and evidence rather more widely than had been the case previously. This was very necessary as activity was starting to pick up in these post-war years and there was a huge number of lettings and lease renewals to be handled for which a good knowledge of available market evidence was essential, in addition to seemingly endless repair work and work upon the still many outstanding cases of war damage compensation.

This management work was mainly under Kenneth as the Agent to the client, but other urban partners called me away to assist them as well: perhaps to give me some variety but also, probably, to assess how I was shaping up. Sam asked me to help him with a compensation case, in which our client's property, Ben's Cafe, a little green timber pull up for carmen standing roughly where now lies one of the main runways of Heathrow Airport, was being acquired by the Airports Authority. I cannot now remember the details of the case but I sat in Sam's room when a representative of the purchasing Authority came in, sat down opposite Sam at his desk, slapped down a dossier about an inch thick and started to read from the first page. Sam bore this with visibly mounting impatience for about three pages and then said 'I must interrupt you. Which page is your valuation on?' 'I am coming to that in due course.' 'Yes, but which page is it on?' 'Well,' the visitor replied, 'it comes at the end after I have explained my case to you.' 'I know your case,' said Sam, 'could you now please move to the page containing your valuation.' The poor man's programme thus disrupted, the meeting was finished in record time.

The other partner who took an interest in me was Jack Wix. He had been the junior partner, just before the war, of a sole practitioner in Victoria Street and had come to the firm with his boss when the latter agreed to amalgamate in order to meet the expressed wish of the then named Ecclesiastical Commissioners that the partnership should be strengthened at the top. This request, which had to be taken seriously, followed departures at the top that left Richard Trumper, the father of Peter, and Kenneth as the only two remaining partners and both only in their upper thirties. As it happened, the new senior partner died almost immediately and Jack went to war where he was captured in the Western Desert. On his return he concentrated largely upon the smaller urban and general clients of the firm. One of these clients had a chairman who was also in the chair of a furniture retailer with shops all over the North of England. This chain employed an over enthusiastic property manager who considered one of his priorities to be to maximize the street trading frontages of his shops by cutting away any structures that appeared, to his eyes, to restrict them. This led to the sensational collapse of a multi-storey building in the Midlands in the middle of a busy shopping morning.

The chairman called for one of our building surveyors to make immediate safety checks of all his shops and also asked Jack to inspect and value them. I was asked to be his assistant for this task, which involved several tours of inspections sandwiched, rather like my trips to South Wales a little earlier, between other work in London. Jack was eighteen years my senior and we got on well as a team for this work although, here again, I realized that there was little checking of evidence of values on the ground and the values were, in consequence, probably lower than they should have been. However, for me these outings were important as it was evident subsequently that Jack had formed a good opinion of what capabilities I had during this work and was the partner, two years later, who insisted that it was in the long term interests of the business to secure me to the partnership sooner rather than later.

I was not alone among my younger colleagues in thinking that the firm had to learn new post-war practices and that, in particular, it had to move to a more commercial stance, both to be better informed and to achieve the higher profit margins that could be earned from what was known as 'agency' work, that is, buying, selling, letting and investing. This work was of course already being done, but largely within the ring fenced managed estates. In time this wider approach was accepted, but it took time. When we amalgamated with a small firm in 1960 that conducted property auctions I recall a solemn debate at a partners' meeting as to whether sales by auction were compatible with Cluttons' professional image! Fortunately the younger element carried the day, supported, I must say, by at least some of the seniors. However, agreeing to be more commercial was one thing; achieving it was another. The agricultural side of the business made some progress against not too formidable opposition but on the urban side we were competing for work and clients that were already well served by big firms that had entered these markets much earlier. Progress was therefore slower and this unfortunately led to some strains later on.

All that was some way in the future and for the present people like me were busy enough in doing the work that had been allotted to us. Life was not all work however and I soon became involved in contacts with others like myself in other firms, firstly through social dining and secondly through the RICS itself. I had obtained my qualification as a Chartered Surveyor in the summer of 1953 and later that year was invited to join, or rather become a founder member of, my first surveyors' dining club. These clubs, of which there are several, play a valuable and enjoyable role in bringing surveyors together socially rather than only over the negotiating table. When subsequently one does have to discuss business matters with a fellow member, it oils the wheels to be acquainted with him, to the client's eventual benefit. I had not been long qualified before I was asked to represent my London branch of the Institution on the RICS Junior Organization and to become its honorary secretary. This brought me into contact with young surveyors all over the country, through regular meetings in London and on branch visits that it was my job to make in company with the chairman for the year. My employers encouraged me in this as they thought that it would be good both for me and for the firm. They were right on both counts as I made a great many friends, some of them life long, and my contacts throughout the country were of assistance later on when I needed market information for regular valuation work. I was secretary for three years and, later, chairman for one and I would not have missed it all for worlds.

Back again to 1953, matters still more vital to my future

happiness were evolving. In the course of my meeting with Jill at the swimming party and our subsequent cinema visit, the usual exploratory conversation on these occasions soon revealed that there were now no impediments to our enjoying one another's company and it was not long before I took my courage in both hands and asked her out again. Courtships were conducted in a very polite way by the apparent standards of today, and certainly very innocently, but this perhaps only contributed to the intoxicating effect that they produced. Suffice it to say, it was a period of unimagined happiness to us both and in May 1954 Jill made the rash decision to accept my proposal and we dashed down to a jeweller in Brighton's East Street where we found an attractive ring that we could just afford from the second-hand tray, as my finances certainly would not have run to the price tags on the new ones. In fact it was only through the generosity of my Godmother's bequest, plus the gifts of family and friends at our wedding, that we were able to contemplate setting up house at all. We were both still earning very little and were well aware that neither of our parents had much to spare. But happiness is not measured by cash in the bank and we were very happy indeed!

Matters moved on apace. Jill celebrated her twenty first birthday in July and we were able to persuade the local coal merchant and part time property developer to grant us a tenancy of a semi-detached house in a close in Haywards Heath, conveniently accessible to the railway station as the estate agent would say and with a generous garden, all in an attractive location and all for £66 a year! We had to go and beard this rather rough diamond in his fuel ordering office to ask him about the house, having heard through some grapevine that the existing tenant was about to move out. He said nothing, so to keep the conversation flowing I said, in what I hoped was a tactful manner, 'I suppose there is a waiting list?' He looked us up and down again, then said 'Well yes, there is (pause) but you can 'ave it if you want it.' The fact that Jill's father was the town clerk, with whom this man sometimes had to deal, probably had something to do with it, but for us it was another joyous milestone that enabled us to be married at St Wilfrid's Church, Haywards Heath, in September and to live happily ever after – as the reader will see if I can keep this up for long enough!

To begin with though things hardly went as planned. We escaped too much ribaldry, tin cans or candy floss on the Morris Minor that was now our car, or kippers on the engine, by being whisked from the reception in a taxi to the car which was hidden in a friend's garage, allowing us to be on our way to Southampton airport in the naive belief that no one would detect that we were newly weds. In fact, it must have been pretty obvious and we were to get some good humoured banter before what proved to be a very long night was over. We soon realized that our flight to Jersey might not leave on time because it was getting quite foggy. Our next discovery was that the small passenger lounge at the airport offered no food and only Lucozade to drink. Thus we spent the first few hours of our honeymoon stuck in a very public lounge, where we were conspicuous in our smart and obviously new going away clothes, no doubt with a few bits of confetti still clinging to them, consuming large quantities of gaseous drink on increasingly empty stomachs. At some late point in the evening, plane delay announcements were changed to one that told us that all flights had been cancelled and that a bus would take Channel Islands passengers to the steamer ferry. We had of course no cabin booking so we sat in the ship's lounge all night while sympathetic fellow passengers made comments of the 'isn't it a shame' variety and one, who had probably found a drink supply that had escaped us, kept referring to us as 'Harold Lloyd and his lady'. I suppose the horn rimmed glasses that I

At St Wilfred's Church, Haywards Heath, 18 September 1954.

wore at the time gave me a passing resemblance. When we found this character on the beach a few days later he had sobered up and effected not to recognize us.

By the time that the ship served breakfast while calling at St Peter Port harbour we fell upon it with enthusiasm, oblivious of Jill's smudged make up and my incipient beard. When we finally reached our hotel towards midday we fell straight into bed, shared for the first time together, far too tired even for lunch and certainly for any other celebration of the occasion.

CHAPTER 8

Junior Partner

W E WERE very happy in our first home. With wedding presents and my Godmother's kindness we were able to start out more or less fully furnished, which would have taken us time to achieve otherwise. At the time of our marriage I was earning about £650 a year and Jill was paid £3 a week as an assistant teacher in a school of dancing in Haywards Heath. I added another £3 to this and we must have lived quite happily on a housekeeping outlay of £6 a week. When I was summoned to see my senior urban partner cousin, Kenneth, in the office one day in the Spring of 1955 to be told that I was to be admitted into partnership from the first of May, I thought he said that I could expect an income, as a share of profits, of £750 a year. I did not find that as exciting as I had expected but thought I should, nevertheless, express my gratitude, which I did. In fact, he had said 'eleven, fifty' and in the event it was quite a good year and my share of profits came to about £2,500. The result was that within a year of our marriage we were really quite well off and had money to spare, a part of which I used to buy a kit from which to build my first boat, a sailing dinghy of the Osprey class.

My grandfather, John Henry, whose leisure activity was trawling for fish, had been a member of both the Royal Temple Yacht Club at Ramsgate, where he kept his boat, and, confusingly, the Royal Thames Yacht Club in London where he worked. He put my father in as a member of both clubs shortly after the end of the war in 1918, although as I have recorded, it was not until the mid-1930s that my father had the money with which to buy a boat of his own – alas, a pleasure of short duration. He, in turn, was keen for his sons to follow the tradition, and interest in the sea, and to this end sent me to stay in the Royal Temple at Ramsgate, after the end of my last Tonbridge term in 1947, to crew with one of his friends during the school summer holiday period and to learn to be a sailor. My grandfather had been commodore of the club, which still displayed trophy cups that he had donated, and my father also had retained his membership for many years. I, in turn, was made a member that summer and was taught to sail Essex One Design dinghies and to help crew them during a memorable holiday for which I have always been grateful. On the strength of that experience I was put up for membership of the Royal Thames in London, as a cadet member at the subscription of two guineas a year! My father and I both gave up our memberships at Ramsgate when there was no longer any likelihood of either of us making any further use of them, but he continued with the Thames until his death and I have to date clocked up some fifty five years. I have never been the 'clubbable' member that my father was, partly because I saw how much it cost him to prop up the bar with his friends almost every evening after work and before coming home, but also because, while I have enjoyed my membership, my priority was always to get home to my family. Nevertheless, it was good to feel that, privileged to be a member of so illustrious a yacht club, I actually had a boat of my own to sail even though my new wife was not exactly an enthusiastic crew member, despite trying hard to like it!

The partnership of which I was invited to become a member was now ten in number and it may set the scene to say a little about those who, of necessity, must be mentioned again in the course of this short history. The senior partner was Richard

Trumper, who had succeeded his father William in that role. William had been my grandfather's principal assistant in his agricultural management work and the Trumpers were still on that rural side of the business. Richard had recently been the youngest president of the RICS and was still spending much of his time on Institution affairs. He was to be less and less in London, leaving the heading of the business effectively to Kenneth and making his contribution by supervising agricultural estates in the West Country and from an associated office at Exeter, near to where he had his country home. He retired completely in 1960 at age sixty. My second cousin Kenneth Marr-Johnson was four years his junior and effectively the joint senior partner, with ultimate responsibility for the whole of the firm's urban business that comprised over two thirds of the total and a rather higher proportion of average profitability.

The next three partners making up the senior profit sharing group were my other second cousin Cecil (Sam), Jack Wix and a delightful former senior assistant on the agricultural side, Harold Hinge. Harold came from a farming family in Kent and was a longstanding friend of Jack whose father had been a solicitor at Faversham. The remaining five were recent additions in 1953 and at a more 'junior' profit sharing level. A few years earlier the partners had received a bad jolt when two key managers left to take up senior posts elsewhere. One of these was William Bishop who was offered the senior partnership of Drivers Jonas. This loss forced the partners to realize that partnership could no longer be restricted mainly to the two leading families and that this status had to be offered to other key managers upon whom the day to day work of the urban business depended. Thus four of the new five were promoted senior urban surveyors; all very competent and experienced people of the kind that could have expected to be partners in smaller practices long since but whose loyalty to the firm, where most of them had started as boys in the Hall, was unquestioned.

The fifth of the most recent intake was Peter Trumper, son of Richard, then about twenty nine and not long returned from land agency training with a firm in Northumberland. I learned later that the urban seniors had hoped to keep Peter and me more or less level pegging for the sake of the future but this was not really possible in view of the differences in our ages at the time. Another factor was that William Trumper had died and left his capital in the firm to his grandson. As Jack put it to me, whom I think he regarded as his protegée, 'We had to make him a partner before you. He has more money in the firm than any of us!'

Partnership status did not for some time make much difference to my work. I came in with one other, Leonard Simpkins. He was eight years older than me and was working under Sam on urban managements for clients, including the Church Commissioners, mainly in western London. I gathered that Leonard had been Sam's nominee; he, Sam, feeling that I was still too young. Jack on the other hand stressed his own opinion that I had what it took, despite my age, and that the firm needed to show the Church in particular that family succession was taking place. There was thus a compromise and both Leonard and I joined the team at the bottom of the heap and at a new, and lowest, profit sharing level. Leonard was a good surveyor and a good friend but in time one had to agree that Jack had been right. Leonard did not exert himself too strenuously and he and his wife, with no family, had as their main interest in life training and following horses. I was only made an equity, as opposed to salaried, partner at such an early age because the firm had recently taken on a new accountant and tax adviser who maintained that a salaried partner, which had normally been the first rung of the ladder, was a contradiction in terms. Despite this purist and accountancy view, the time came again when we needed people to be given 'partner' status but did not wish to expand equity ownership to the numbers that this implied, so that the normal practice was resumed. I was therefore a lucky exception to have been a 'full' partner for, as it turned out, thirty seven years; a longer term than most of my predecessors and my successors. If there was an advantage it was that I was able to see and be part of the workings of the partnership from an early age and, even if I was not expected to express my opinions too frequently at first, the long apprenticeship was valuable to me later on.

The firm that I had joined is one of the three or four oldest in the surveying profession. Our branch of the Clutton family arrived in Sussex from Cheshire, where our origins can be traced back to the time of the Conquest, when my four greats grandfather Ralph, who was a younger son and did not therefore inherit the family estates, took Holy Orders and was appointed to the incumbencies of Horsted Keynes and Portslade. Most of the family then either entered the Church or, if female, either married parsons or kept house for bachelor parson brothers. One who did not follow the trend was my three greats grandfather, William, the youngest of four brothers, who took employment with a land agent and timber merchant at Cuckfield, married his daughter and was in effective control of the business by 1765, when he was issuing accounts in his own name. He, in turn, bought an estate south of Reigate for his surveyor son, another William, and the largely land agency business was conducted from there, from what was also the family home, for the next century and a quarter. In the 1830s the firm was instructed to purchase land for the construction of the South Eastern Railway and this railway work made it necessary, in time, to have a London office which was opened in Whitehall Place by my great grandfather, John, in 1837. He was phenomenally successful so that, while still in partnership with his brothers, both in Sussex and in London where they helped him out from time to time, he had established within a decade or so what became a separate and much larger business based upon the expanding railway work – particularly in arbitrating disputes – and on advising two of the major landowners of that time and this, the Ecclesiastical Commission, now the Church Commissioners, and the Commissioners of Woods and Forests, now the Crown Estate. The firm also had smaller clients, what were called in the accounts 'Casual Business', one of which was Henry Smith's Charity; a small client then but one that was to grow in importance later on. John, the first President of what was then the Surveyors' Institution, left the London business to his three surveyor sons, one of whom was my grandfather, John Henry, while the Reigate firm passed to his nephew before the family involvement ceased. That firm now practises from East Grinstead.

The partnership of twelve was small enough in numbers for all partners to know one another quite well and similarly for our wives through the social dances and other occasions run as annual fixtures by the RICS. There were good relations with the main clients, all of whom seemed to be secure, and business arrangements with them were mostly based upon the fee scales laid down either by the Institution or by other statutory bodies, with little need to compete for business by competitive quotes and with few, if any, clients having thought of the current practice of holding 'beauty parades' at regular intervals. We all worked hard, or at least the younger ones did although some of the older were beginning to ease off, and we did our best to maintain the best possible professional standards. Life was therefore secure, substantially stress free, and rewarding to an extent that precluded financial worries, in a partnership atmosphere that was rather like that of a club. It did not last of course. In time the numbers had to increase as the firm diversified and also opened branch offices, while life became steadily more competitive and the profit margins less predictable. For the first part of my professional career I was nevertheless very lucky to be working with such people and in such an environment.

I was also fortunate in another way; one that afforded interest and variety to my working life. The firm's work in the fifties was still largely the management of urban and country estates. There were therefore departments of specialists necessary to this work, such as building surveyors and architects and people skilled in war damage claim work and some aspects of Town and Country Planning, in addition to the estate management teams. Other specializations that are the norm today, such as teams dealing with valuation, rating, investment, sales and lettings, were however lacking as there was thought to be no need for them. Estate Managers, for example, regarded themselves as the experts on their particular patches and would have resented any suggestion that they needed to call in a specialist for any of what they regarded as their management functions. Therefore, when a client wanted the firm to act in a case requiring one of these other functions, the younger partners were usually given the task and were expected to teach themselves how to do it, perhaps supervised by a more senior partner whose experience of the particular function might however, through lack of much direct experience, have been equally minimal. Later on our efforts to diversify the business and the growth of what I might call non-management instructions led us to set up a number of specialist departments, staffed by those trained and experienced in the particular functions. For many years as a junior partner however, I and others, both urban and rural, were fortunate in having our regular management tasks interrupted from time to time by other instructions which not only made a welcome change but which also forced us to learn fast as well as enabling us to travel to and to get to know towns in parts of the country to which our management tasks never took us.

This, of course, was not an ideal arrangement and the clients were sometimes less well served than they would now be by these jobs being done by specialists. When, as sometimes happened, I was told to arrange the sale of someone's country house – there then being no estate agency within the firm – I did all the proper advertising, preparation of particulars and so on but in retrospect I am not at all sure that I obtained the highest price that might have been on offer because I had no real knowledge of that particular market. On another occasion a friend of one of my senior partners was a trustee of an approved school in the Lake District and I was sent to inspect and to agree a sale to the Local Authority to which it was to be handed over. I found an old stone mill converted into a school and home for a number of boys and, with my commercial management background, such as it was, did my sums as to likely value for conversion to some form of industrial use; there being no demand for approved schools in the market as far as I could see. I then went to see the District Valuer acting for the purchasers to find that his alternative value assumed demolition and the building of a number of holiday homes! As it happened we had, by these quite different routes, arrived at about the same sale price. I was so impressed by the rightness of his approach that I felt bound to agree without further ado. The client in due course was perfectly happy, but I had a nagging feeling afterwards that I should have argued for something better. I thought then of a quote attributed to my great grandfather who, when asked by a pushy Counsel at a land dispute hearing 'Mr Clutton, do you never make mistakes?' replied 'Yes, more than most men. But then I do more business than most men'. It did not really make me feel much better.

I have always felt a distaste for argument over money; even

my client's money, and have recognized that, for a negotiator, I am rather too ready to see the other side's point of view, particularly if it is well argued. In discussing matters of value I had to steel myself to an attitude of toughness that I did not always feel and which, I like to think, was not entirely in character. The client, however, had the right to expect the best possible deal and one had to adopt the attitude best fitted to securing it. It was not always so. When I first started, most of our major client reports ended with words such as 'We recommend these terms as a fair and reasonable settlement'; the maintenance of good relations as between landlord and tenant being regarded as just as important as the terms of a financial transaction. Alas, the number of clients wishing to be told that something is fair and reasonable, while they still exist, have been overtaken in number by those wanting to be convinced that the orange has been squeezed dry! In time, when I was involved in many deals for a number of clients, I became used to haggling but I always tried, by homework in advance, to be convinced, by the evidence and by the arithmetic, of the justification for the most advantageous line of argument that I felt could be adopted and supported. The advance homework took the form of permutating the possible approaches in order to find the best that could reasonably be maintained. By this means I felt able to argue logically, rather than simply aggressively or with bluster, from the basis of what I hoped was sound preparation. I kept my records of the permutations on file and I was glad that I had done so when visited by a formidable lady from the Treasury, to which the Crown Estate reported, who wanted to see evidence on this very point as to the research and consideration of alternatives that lay behind the firm's advice to the Estate. My clients were always naturally concerned, when the Treasury were doing one of their periodic inquiries of this nature, that they would not suffer the embarrassment of the agents upon whose

Our first home, a three bed 'semi' with large garden, all for £66 a year!

advice they relied being found wanting. On this occasion I think the report must have been satisfactory because I was pleased to be thanked later on by the Chairman for my cooperation, as indeed was the other principal London agent concerned. He and I often exchanged views, so as to ensure that no one could try to drive a wedge between us to the detriment of our mutual client.

My business visit to the Lake District was an eye opener to a landscape that, up until then, I had hardly known existed. Later, when we were invited there by a surveyor friend, Bill Elias, we were to start a lifelong love of what became a favourite holiday destination, even though originally it took a gruelling twelve hour car journey to get there. This friend was one of those made in the course of the RICS Junior Organization meetings that I have mentioned. His practice was in Liverpool but in the war his father had leased a house in Troutbeck, by Windermere, to which his family could be sent to escape the worst of the bombing. In the mid 1950s it came up for auction and Bill was able to buy what amounted almost to a small estate for the maximum that he could scrape together; about £2,500 as I recollect. That was the time at which to invest, but not all of us could see ahead and few of us had the means even if we could!

The Junior Organization Committee met monthly at the RICS headquarters in London and was made up of members from each of the London and Provincial branches, including those in Scotland and Eire. These were enjoyable occasions at which we discussed matters that we at least thought to be of great moment but we also had a number of social events. By virtue of my appointment as honorary secretary, I was required, as I have said, to accompany the chairman for the year to each of the provincial branches in the course of his chairmanship, so that I was in a position to get to know everyone better than most in the course of these perambulations. Several of these visits were for dinners or dances to which I could take Jill, and we had some wonderful fun in the years before family commitments made it less easy for her to stay away from home although, through the kindness of her mother as a baby sitter, she did manage one or two events in the year, later on, when it became my turn to take the National chair.

It was not until many years later, when I was undertaking regular valuation work around the country, that I appreciated one of the unexpected benefits of all these friendships which was that they gave me an entrée to firms from which I needed local market information. I asked only for factual market evidence; not for any guidance as to the resultant deductions as to value, and I made a practice of allocating a part of Clutton's fee in each case to be paid to those firms who had been able to provide useful data. These were not of course my only sources but they certainly helped in the initial stages of this work when the firm's agency (in the sense of buying and selling commercial property) activities and the data bases that they supported were still in their infancy. Not all sources of information were from friends known to me. I once called upon a leading surveyor in a county town who was very helpful and to whom I said when I thanked him that there would be a modest cheque in the post. He replied that he had had his brain picked by visiting London agents for as long as he could remember and that this was the first time that anyone had offered to share a fee! While this source of market data was useful, it was not unknown to find that agents on the spot were not aware of deals done by London agents in their towns. These sources had to be checked as well, as far as it could be done. Fortunately, these main agents, or their clients, liked to issue press announcements of deals and it was only the most uncooperative agent who refused the detail of such transactions when asked for them. When it came to needing evidence for any purpose, we were really all in the same boat.

To return again to the earlier years, Peter Trumper's maternal grandfather had been secretary to the Missions to Seamen, on the strength of which the firm was asked to advise on the buying, selling and maintenance of a number of staff houses round the country, plus building works to many of their seamen's missions in the ports. The latter work was done by a building surveyor colleague but the houses were passed to me. It turned out to be a breath of fresh air for me but a somewhat expensive and unnecessary way in which to look after these tasks and after a few years the client employed an internal surveyor to do the work. Not before, however, I had turned up to a house in Hartlepool driving my first office car, a brand new Ford Consul of which I was particularly proud, only to be greeted by the strong Yorkshire accent of the man who opened the door saying

'I 'ope we are not paying for that!' It was an early lesson as to how, while a professional should not convey an appearance of being so bad at his job as not to be reasonably turned out, neither should one appear to be doing too well out of the client. When he asked me where I had stayed the night I did not dare to say that the local hotel, having few other guests, had put me in the very splendid bridal suite.

Jobs like that one were a chance to get out of London from time to time but they also meant leaving my new wife for sometimes several days on end so when we were first married and also when the children were small I was happier with my main work as a junior partner, which was in London and allowed me to be home at night. This work had now extended, following the retirement of 'Charlie', to the supervision, under Kenneth for the management and Jack for some of the development situations, of most of the commercial estates in Inner London owned by the Church Commissioners, including the ones where I had previously been the junior assistant. One of my first tasks on returning to Cluttons had been to prepare, at the request of my elder cousin, a map of Central London to show the extent and proximity to one another of all the managements in our charge. I still have it and it is strange now to be reminded of just how much ground we covered between about six urban management teams. Strange, because commercial property portfolios today tend to be composed of individually built or selected large blocks of offices, factory estates and shopping centres; high on value but comparatively low on land area on the map. In the years soon after the war's end many of the larger estates occupied substantial areas on the map, being made up, as some still are today, of a large number of properties in ring fence ownership, with a majority of properties let on ground leases where the freehold estate owner received, sometimes for many years yet to come, only a fixed

Following the auctioneer at the Church Commissioners' auction of
'fixed interest' properties, January 1963. (L to R) W.R. Paice,
Church Surveyor; Jack Wix and Rafe Clutton of Cluttons and
Sir Hubert Ashton, Church Estates Commissioner.

ground rent bearing no relationship with the actual value of the
property.

The Commissioners were under new management at the top
and there was pressure to pursue, for the property holdings, the
change of emphasis from fixed interest to equity investment that
had already been substantially achieved within their Stock
Exchange portfolios. As well therefore as trying, so far as
building licensing controls allowed, to catch up with a
considerable backlog of repairs for those properties where this
was the freeholder's responsibility – and chasing lessees to do so
where it was not – as well as dealing with a multitude of claims
in respect of war damage, we also had to try, in so far as we

could, to effect switches from ground rental income to rack rents, or at least improved ground rents, that could be reviewed to reflect changes in value of the underlying properties and, by implication, keep up with inflation when this began to become an important consideration later on. These processes, that implied reaching acceptable agreement with the head leaseholders in question, could not be hurried, other than at the cost of doing a less favourable deal, and in many cases it was not possible to do anything at all. However, our clients were in a hurry, one consequence of which was that we were instructed to sell many vacant sites because the fact that they were not productive of income was perceived as an embarrassment. As a result of enemy action there were many of these on the fringes of the City of London, in locations that were yet to benefit from the first post-war construction boom that was to occur later. Several fledgling but far sighted property developers were able to base their later fortunes on the advantageous acquisition of development sites at this time from owners who, for one reason or another, did not feel able to wait for the market to improve. The client took the same view of the larger commercial buildings that were let on long leases at fixed ground rents. These included many impressive central London blocks that we were instructed to sell in conjunction with one of the big commercial firms acting as auctioneers and joint agents with us. In aggregate value of lots, this auction, held in 1963, was the largest that had been experienced up to that time. The Commissioners were pleased with the prices obtained, which reflected the purchasers' perception of the huge long term potential of the lease reversions. It is debatable whether the Clients should not have held on for these reversionary benefits themselves but, in fairness, these were difficult to quantify at the time whereas the prices obtained and reinvested must have given a welcome and immediate income increase over the former ground rents. The new income also met the imperative for this to be of an equity nature and not fixed.

Not all vacant sites were sold. Some of the best sites, or holdings where there were buildings but where the vacant site would represent the higher value, were kept for development assembly within the freeholder's control but, when the boom started, other development opportunities had to be created by much patient acquisition of interests existing within the potential development sites. There were many of these within our management, the largest of all being the five and a half acre Paternoster site north of St Paul's Cathedral. Although largely derelict, this area still contained a number of occupied buildings outstanding on lease, including two department stores and a number of shops and residential flats, as well as offices. It fell to me and my able assistant to clear all of these by negotiation as best we could and at the least possible cost. It was a wearing task indeed since, although there were vague suggestions that the City Corporation would use compulsory purchase powers in the last resort, no actual powers were available and we were working to a not unlimited timetable. Our clients, who had already set up a development consortium, had agreed to let it the main site on a reviewable ground rent representing a stated percentage return upon whatever it cost to assemble the site – my senior partner's representations as to reference to market value having been overruled in the interests of harmony within the consortium, of which the Commissioners were a major shareholder and also because it was a very large investment and the range of uncertainties had to be limited to achieve agreement at all. Eventually we completed the acquisitions and reported the total outlay to our clients, consoling ourselves with the thought that at least there would be a rent of the agreed percentage of that cost, even if the true value of the site were higher. When we heard that a final grand gesture had been made of rounding the rent down to a rather lower figure my assistant and I could only go out and console ourselves with several stiff drinks!

Some of these site assembly operations were really quite difficult as there was the potential for almost anyone with any sort of interest to hold the freeholder to ransom. One therefore had to use a lot of tact and frequently turn the other cheek. A leaseholder of a shop selling beanstalk shelving in the City Road would only talk to me in the bar of the Grosvenor Hotel at Victoria Station on his way home in the evening and I had many a session when I should have been well on my own way home to my wife and young family. Needless to say in the circumstances, the drinks were always on me! In another case, where the clearance had to be done by the lessee developer and not, for once, by ourselves on behalf of the freeholder, the owner of an Italian restaurant was the only tenant left on a major site in the City. It had reached the point at which the developers were seeking consents for a scheme revision that would allow them to build their new office block round the obstruction when the man finally gave in, leaving the country that same evening with a large suitcase full of used notes.

In most cases the Church Commissioners took the precaution of letting development sites to development companies, rather than taking on the direct development risk themselves. They then became shareholders in the joint development company formed with their developer lessee and usually also lent a part, or even the whole, of the finance required. This arrangement was supposed to mean that the developer, and not the freeholder, took the risk; and so it turned out when things were booming, but the time was to come when this system was shown to be flawed. Several smaller developments were however undertaken directly and we then found ourselves organizing the whole operation, from site clearance, through setting up and managing the consultancy team and building tenders, etc., to eventual letting of the completed new or improved building on behalf of the client. Thus passed my first decade or so of partnership, originally working from the firm's head office in Westminster and then, from 1959 for about eight years, from a small office that we opened in the City of London in order to be closer to our managements and also so that Kenneth could achieve a long held ambition of acting as surveyor to one of the Great Twelve City livery companies; it being expected at the time that this implied working from a City address. My father, who had worked in the City all his life said 'There is only one piece of good advice that I give to anyone contemplating working in the City. Never eat curry on a Monday'.

CHAPTER 9

Life in the Main Stream

O UR SON OWEN was born in 1958, when we were still living at our first home in Haywards Heath. I 'phoned my parents to announce the new arrival and my father asked me what we were going to call him. 'Owen,' I replied, thinking that it would please him that we had chosen a name used many times in our family history. 'That's appropriate,' he said. 'I've been owin' all my life.' Jill's parents lived in the next residential close to ours, a quarter of a mile away, so they were able to see the baby and watch his progress almost daily, Jill having by this time given up her work as a dancing teacher. As her parents had no other family ours were able to benefit for the whole of their childhood from the undivided attention of their maternal grandparents living never more than a quarter of an hour's drive away.

My parents had moved from the family home at Ardingly at about the time of our marriage. The house and large garden had rapidly been getting too much for them with the departure of the family in various directions, either upon marriage, to live with friends or, in my case, for a short time to a flat in Haywards Heath. My parents had to cope with a substantial claim for dilapidations under the terms of the lease of the old house but they were able, now that they only had to house themselves, to move to the inexpensive little bungalow at Pevensey Bay that my mother had bought in the thirties for some few hundred pounds and in which we had had many a family holiday. The relief of at last living in an establishment well within their means was obvious and they were very happy there despite the limited floor space. Later, they bought a slightly larger house right on the edge of the shingle beach at the other end of the village and we used to load up the family car and make regular weekend visits, both to see my parents and to swim in the sea only a stone's throw, and at high tide much less, away.

In 1959 we felt able, after one or two 'good' years in terms of partnership profits, to buy our first house. We wanted to be in the country and the choice fell to a modest house in an acre of garden in the village of Plumpton. What we did not realize was that a former owner had had an old orchard removed by bulldozer, taking much of the topsoil with it. Our ambitions of starting a real garden proved therefore to be restricted to not much more than grass, roses and potatoes on the heavy Sussex clay that lay only just below the surface. Another effect of the clay was that the house moved up and down according to the season, with doors tending to stick at the top for one half of the year and at the bottom for the other; a typical surveyor's house! Actually, our predecessor but one had been a local surveyor friend and the house next door was the home of a building surveyor from one of the London firms. I don't recollect that his doors stuck but he certainly had the same problems that we did of heavy clay and occasionally, when the clay was saturated, of overflowing drainage systems, so it was nice to think that I was not the only surveyor to be better, I liked to hope, at looking after his clients' interests in these respects than his own!

Despite all this we were very happy in the first home that was really our own. It is still there, now considerably enlarged, so the clay effects can't have been too bad. For our first few months we were often called to the telephone by local traders wanting to know where our immediate predecessors had gone; apparently it had been some time since they had paid anyone's bills. It was only then that we realized that they had given us no forwarding

address, which was not altogether surprising given their
expectation, no doubt, that the only post was likely to be from
creditors, as well as possibly fearing what we might say to them
about the condition in which they had left the house had we
known where they were. I have heard of vendors removing light
bulbs but I had not previously come across ones who removed
the fittings as well!

Our second son, Gareth, was born in this house and the dash
to get back there in time from London was one of those
experiences that one never forgets. It was at the time of one of
our national fuel crises and Jack Wix had just bought a petrol
saving, and minute, three wheeled bubble car which he had
driven over to our City office. I received a 'phone call in the
early afternoon to tell me that the baby was starting and my
partner told our commissionaire to use the car to get me as
quickly as possible to the train at Victoria station. My driver took
the urgency to heart and drove at breakneck speed through the
traffic, which I endured a few inches behind the large plastic
bubble and at a level from the street not much more than half
way up the wheels of the buses round which we dodged. It may
well have been about then that my hair started to turn white. It
certainly felt like it.

It was when, a few years later, that one of my partners, a man
of private means, invited me in to his spacious home in
Hampstead to change for a dinner we were both attending that I
remember thinking 'I am just as good a surveyor as he is. Why
therefore am I living in such a small house when he is in such a
large one!' The short answer was that he was wealthier than I
was, but the thought spurred me to think about more living
space. We liked the country surroundings, although we have
never been into country pursuits as such, and we had harboured
an ambition to live beside the Chailey Common in Mid Sussex,
an area of some four hundred and fifty acres of heathland. We

could not find a house to buy but we were able, in the summer of 1961, to discover that a local builder was to develop an estate of six houses – four smaller and two larger ones, the latter bordering upon and facing south across the common. We made frequent trips to watch the progress of building; exciting when things were happening but frustrating when often they were not. Eventually, our new home was finished and we moved in on the last day of May, 1962, accompanied by just enough furniture to make the essential rooms barely habitable. It was an ideal family home and, with extensions as the family grew, we were to be there for a third of a century, with our sons Jonathan and Niall born in the house, where our daughter Helen would also have been born had not the powers that be, regarding Jill as an 'older' mother-to-be at the grand age of thirty four, insisted that Cuckfield Hospital should have that honour.

Fathers had not generally been welcomed in the delivery room – at least not by our midwives – for our first births, but things were more relaxed for the last two. The arrival of our daughter took place in the middle of the night and during one of the noisiest thunderstorms that I can remember. The midwife, a large, coal black lady, said to Jill sternly 'Now, I hope that you are not going to scream' and then told me to operate the gas and air machine. It was only when it was all over that I realized that to make any gas come out I should have pressed a button on the side. However, the psychological effect seemed to have done the trick and I had no complaints.

We enjoyed putting our roots down in the first home that we felt to be permanent and we soon became part of the community. Jill was a founder member of the local W.I., to which she still belongs, and we were both involved in the Society that was formed by a local naturalist to see to the conservation of the Commons prior to their becoming, firstly, registered common land and, later on, a Site of Special Scientific Interest. I sang in the Church choir and got elected to, and later chaired, the Parish Council, and spent some fourteen years as a churchwarden. I was expected to exercise my surveying knowledge, such as it was, so I searched diligently for woodworm and found quite a lot of it, which led to a treatment specialist coming in to spray the floors that supported the pews. I had not appreciated that a flower festival was due shortly afterwards and I was in the dog house for a while when the flowers all drooped and the Matins service had to be abandoned half way through because no one could tolerate the smell. On the plus side, the evidence of active woodworm did not reappear. Someone arranged for a group of trusty prisoners from Lewes prison to form a working party to clear up the churchyard. I supervised the work during one Saturday, with my two younger boys keeping me company. At the end of the day I thanked the men, when one of them said 'In fact, it is we who should be thanking you.' When I said something like 'No, not at all,' he said 'You brought your children along and we really appreciate that. People don't realize, but we never see children in prison.' The thought had not occurred to me and I could only think how awful and be glad that I had brought them with me.

In the year in which Owen was born the partners assembled for a conference at Bournemouth to consider the fact that, for the first time in the firm's existence, the work known to be secured as at the first day of the accounting year would not produce income sufficient to cover the estimated year's outgoings. Income from regular estate management instructions is by its nature more predictable and certain than fees earned in the course of a year as instructions come in and are dealt with. Cluttons had been in the fortunate position, for the whole of the firm's existence, of knowing that, while the level of profit could not be predicted precisely, it was almost impossible for the business actually to make a loss, so long as it could hold on to its management instructions. Such a situation would have been the envy of the majority of our competitors whose businesses were generally less management based, but on the other hand their more risky businesses could be expected, in good years at least, to produce higher profit margins.

The outcome of our discussions, to which one useful contributor was Frank Trumper, first cousin to Richard, the owner of a sole principal and much riskier business with whom we had recently amalgamated, was that we had to enlarge our client base and increase the diversity of the business, with particular emphasis on the market place work of buying, selling and property investment for clients – to which most of us younger ones gave a hearty 'Hear Hear!' This, of course, was easier said than done, although gradually as time went by our dependence on the Church Commissioners was diluted by a variety of new instructions and by the enterprise of some partners who were prepared to teach themselves new tricks. One example of this was the country team who managed to establish a name for the firm in selling country estates and in agricultural investment. Another was the urban partner who taught himself to be a rating surveyor and who secured some valuable clients to the firm for that function.

The other expansion routes that were tried were the acquisition of smaller firms, politely called 'amalgamation', and research into the possibilities of emulating others by opening offices overseas. My partner Jack, who had obtained one or two company non-executive directorships, regarded himself as something of an expert at amalgamations and arranged these with a few smaller firms. The usual common ground was a sole principal whose pension arrangements were inadequate and who, wishing to retire, was happy to hand his firm over to us in return for a paid consultancy for himself plus some modest income guarantee for the rest of his life By this means we secured some useful small clients although, in retrospect, our partner was too kind hearted to be much of a tycoon in these matters, with the result that the person acquired usually did rather better out of the arrangement than we did!

Overseas expansion proved to be much more difficult. Two senior partners toured Canada, having a very interesting and no doubt exhausting time, but with no tangible results other than the making of several friends. Feeling slightly abashed at this, they sent Leonard and me to Australia in 1964, to see why several of our competitors were opening offices there and whether we could do so as well. We also had a most interesting trip and made a number of friends, many of whom promptly called upon us in London in the following years, no doubt to assist them to establish with their Revenue authorities that their world travels were business trips and therefore tax exempt! On our return we prepared and printed a brochure extolling the opportunities for investment in the local property markets and sent copies to our clients. This produced interest and thanks but absolutely no instructions. This was because, as had dawned on us in the course of our visits within Australia, the people who had opened offices had done so on the backs of property company clients for whom they acted here at home and who wished to extend their activities to Australia, as many did for a time. Unfortunately for us, our clients were generally of a different nature and neither willing nor able to invest in the Antipodes. When we did eventually establish ourselves overseas, by opening offices in some of the Gulf States in the mid nineteen seventies, it was to act for local property owners in the management and letting of new constructions rather than for UK clients. We finished our Australian tour as trans-Atlantic passengers on the *Queen Mary* for what must have been approaching her last years of this service and we were both glad to have had that experience. I took to having a swim each morning in the ship's pool which was water heated by letting steam in from the ship's boilers. On my last morning I was earlier than usual and I said to the man in charge 'Steam in yet?' I don't think he heard me and I dived into the coldest water that I have ever experienced! Luckily it was not a large pool and the step ladder was near at hand. Another not to be forgotten experience.

Reverting to amalgamations, the London based land agency partners had for many years used locally based agents to assist in the management of the extensive agricultural estates in their charge. In the locations of the major managed estates we joined with those agents in the formation of local practices bearing the Clutton name together with that or those of the people on the spot. The London firm provided a part of the working capital needed and the more senior partners became partners also in the local firms. The London based appointed agents to the clients continued to bear the ultimate responsibility to the client and to share the fees with the local firms but in due course it suited everybody for these provincial partnerships to become one firm with the parent and for their local partners to become sharing partners, on agreed terms, with those in London. Here again, our 'negotiating' partner failed to realize, or omitted to tell us, that in the year preceding the amalgamation date the provincial firms had done rather well, while London had had a no more than average year. The result was, once again and based on these figures, that the smaller partners to the amalgamation did rather better than the larger ones, at least in the opinions of the younger London partners, although no doubt the provincials felt differently! In a partnership where peace has to be maintained and where therefore there are great pressures for fairness, there is always a tendency when profit shares are being agreed for the element of doubt to benefit the lower sharing bands at the expense of the upper. Thus, whereas the amalgamations achieved the objectives of expanding the business and enlarging the client base by adding the clients that had previously been those of the smaller firms, as well as adding some congenial partners to the practice, mainly in the agricultural division, those of us working to achieve profits in the much larger urban business felt that our representatives had not been over clever!

The next stage in our efforts to expand and diversify came with what was for us a fairly momentous decision to open a commercial agency office in the heart of the market place in Mayfair and to fill it with expensive experts in investment work and in the selling and letting of commercial property – momentous for the reason that the total investment was the largest that the firm had yet undertaken and the income to be expected was quite unpredictable. In fact, there was a good deal of double counting of the projected income benefits as major letting instructions were passed to the specialists, who initially had few instructions of their own, which would otherwise have been dealt with by the management teams, sometimes reinforced by help from specialist joint agents but without any capital outlay by the firm. As it happened, the property market crashed, in conjunction with the oil crisis of the early seventies, within three months of our undertaking this major venture and times were both thin and very worrying for some years to come.

Partnerships are financed in varying ways. During the eighties, when conditions were favourable, several former partnerships, with profit margins high enough to attract investors, floated to become public companies able to attract funds for expansion. This enabled some senior partners, fortunate to be due to retire at these times, to avoid the requirement upon continuing partners to leave their paper goodwill profits in the business and to leave as wealthy people with their shares of the business thus identified and valued for the purposes of the flotation. Cluttons flirted briefly with the valuation of business goodwill a year or two before the outbreak of the war in 1939, due to one partner retiring early on the grounds of ill health and another coming in, with the small firm that he owned, to replace him. Within a year or so both had died and the firm was faced with having to find large sums due to executors from a business the profits of which had been severely reduced by the hostilities. Goodwill was banished from the accounting from that time on and has not reappeared. In our partnership therefore, as in many others, new partners were not required to pay anything to enter the partnership and those leaving were paid nothing for goodwill. There is however a need for partners to provide their business with working capital and this was achieved either by use of private means, for those who had them, or, for most of us, by building up a capital contribution out of income year by year. That investment bore interest and was paid out when the partner retired, needless to say at par. In times of inflation it was not the most attractive form of investment and it will be seen that a firm thus financed had to be careful as to the extent to which it could expand by spending capital.

Partners' own capital was enough until the late 1950s when I was asked by the chief cashier, who did not feel able to approach our austere senior partner himself, to acquaint him with the news that we would be unable to pay staff salaries at the end of the month and to request permission to ask the bank for a loan. As I have mentioned, the senior partner of the firm was still Richard Trumper, who had for some years been living the other side of Exeter, where the Church Commissioners had large estates. For practical purposes my cousin Kenneth fulfilled the role in London so it was to him that I had to go. He was inclined to respond to my requests for advice, second opinion or approbation by saying 'I'm sure you are right', which was complimentary in one way but hardly reassuring when I knew

The partners in 1960. Mentioned in text – Front: (L to R) Cecil (Sam) Clutton, Frank Trumper, Kenneth Marr-Johnson and Jack Wix. Standing: fifth from left, Leonard Simpkins; centre in glasses, Harry Watney (consultant); fourth from right, Peter Trumper; second from right Rafe Clutton.

very well that he had not thought it necessary to examine the subject matter of my approach in any detail. Anyway, it was abundantly clear that nothing would induce him to go cap in hand to our bank manager, so I had to do it. The bank manager expressed surprise that we had managed this long without the facilities that he was used to advancing to similar firms and immediately authorized a 'fall back' overdraft of £20,000. Having thus put a toe into the water, it was not long before a bank facility became a regular supplement to the capital input of the partners and this gave us a little more leeway. It will be seen that financing a business in this way meant that, while the partners hoped to make a reasonable living during their time with the firm, they took nothing out of it afterwards other than what they had themselves put in. As an eponymous partner I always found it slightly galling when clients and others either assumed that I owned the business or at least that I must be well heeled as a successor to my family founders. Alas, while my great grandfather did indeed retire with considerable wealth, from a business that never had a profit margin of less than fifty per cent, his sons in the firm, together with the rest of his family, seemed to have been well able to spend nearly all of it!

While we lacked specialist commercial departments in the sixties, our general reputation did nevertheless attract recommendations for some very interesting assignments. One of these that fell to me – or rather initially to my senior partner but with me and my helpers doing the work – was the task of advising Lambeth Borough Council on a grandiose scheme for redeveloping the whole of Brixton Town Centre, incorporating a kind of park and ride transport interchange designed to keep traffic congestion out of Central London. Schemes of this nature were popular in the sixties but most of them were too ambitious, both in general concept and in the extent of demolition and rebuilding involved, as well as in terms of the sums of public money required on the national planning account in order to achieve them. Brixton was such a concept, on which a lot of work was done but which eventually came to nothing. The main task falling to us, after helping the team with aspects of demand relevant to the designs for the new regional shopping centre and associated commercial and residential new buildings, was to value the whole area for the purpose of drawing up the estimates of costs and rewards. Three partners were involved, together with assistants. In the course of a long and generally hot summer, between us we inspected and measured every building in the town centre area, earning incidentally the largest single-task fee that had ever fallen to the firm. Not all of the shopkeepers were in favour of the idea and one of my partners was physically ejected from two shops! Nevertheless the job was eventually finished and it was disappointing to find afterwards that it had all been a non-starter. The only beneficiary was the District Valuer who seized upon a copy of our valuation workings with alacrity. I only hope they were right! Jobs like these – and there were several, but not so large – provided interesting variety but had to be fitted into my main management responsibilities which were in themselves quite time consuming. I was fortunate in having excellent management assistants, who later became partners and without whom I could not have found time for the many interesting non-management instructions that came my way.

In the early sixties the main part of the huge Paternoster development had been completed, and there came a winter day in its latter stages when a large number of people had been invited to a 'topping out'; the ceremony at which the last piece of building material is added to the highest point of the structure, a task normally undertaken by the chairman of the developer concerned. It was snowing at the time and there was no way that the chairman of the consortium was going to expose his aged frame on a snow covered flat roof many storeys above ground. The answer was for some poor chap who must have drawn the short straw to shovel concrete through the driving snow while the rest of the assembled company watched him via closed circuit television from the comfort of a lower floor that had been temporarily enclosed for the purpose and stocked with lavish refreshments. It was from the uncompleted later stage of this scheme that we had, with our two older boys, a grand stand view of the funeral processions for Sir Winston Churchill, including the arrival of so many dignitaries from other countries who we watched walking up the steps into the western entrance of St Paul's Cathedral.

I was rather taken for a ride over the Paternoster development in one respect. It comprised, as far as I remember, over four hundred thousand square feet of offices, with shops at pedestrian precinct level and car parks and services beneath. The development consortium had pre-let the first and main part of the development in order to limit development risk, two of the main London agents having been instructed. In fact, the tenant was introduced through the friendship of my cousin Kenneth with the chairman of the office occupiers, the Central Electricity Generating Board. One of the agents wrote to thank him, saying that they could not acknowledge the introduction by the usual convention of allocating a part of the letting fee to the introducing agent because this was already having to be shared between two firms. My senior partners, having at that time a lofty but sadly misplaced disdain of commercial agents in general, did not pursue the matter. This same agent was then instructed by the CEGB to sub-let the shops which were not part of their occupation, although included in their lease. Knowing that the Church Commissioners were at that time interested in increasing the retail shopping element of their portfolio, he suggested to me that they might like to take the shopping on a long underlease so that they could then let the individual shops on what appeared to be attractive investment terms. If I, as a young partner, had been watched more closely by a senior with retail experience, or had had that experience myself, I might have been aware, as he certainly must have been, how difficult it would be to let the shops. Things might then have gone differently but, as it was, our clients accepted the suggestion and we became responsible for letting the shopping precinct. This had four main pedestrian approaches and we had no sooner put the shops on the market than one approach was closed to allow the construction of a new entrance to St Paul's Underground station. Another was severely restricted by major roadworks in St Paul's Churchyard. A third entrance was close to a fountain that had been commissioned at considerable expense to stand in the piazza. It was only discovered when it was first turned on that the prevailing wind blew the spray right across the shopping centre approach! With the help of specialist agents who worked very hard upon their retail contacts, we did eventually get the shops let but it was gruelling work and the resulting rents were far below what we had originally expected.

At the beginning of the sixties we thought that we were breaking new ground in negotiating thirty three yearly reviews of the ground rents of the Paternoster leases. In the event, none of these reviews was actually applied as all of the leases had been unscrambled before the review dates were reached. The offices were dated and the tenant wanted to go elsewhere. By the late nineteen eighties the Commissioners were keen to dissolve these joint development arrangements so that they could transfer their investment from taxable income from company dividends to directly received, and untaxed, rents. Their partners had also had enough and were happy to release their interests. There came a time therefore when, by seventeen separate transactions carried out in legal sequence but in practice all on one day and at one sitting of the solicitors concerned, the whole thing was unscrambled and the sites were made available for the attractive and exciting new buildings that have, in 2003, recently been completed to provide, with their new courts and piazzas, a new and far more impressive northern environment to the Cathedral. Soon, few will remember the sixties buildings that received so many criticisms, but for a few of us the trials and tribulations of this first post-war treatment of this important site will not be so easily forgotten! Years later, when one of my jobs was to make regular valuations of retail shops throughout the country for one of the property investment bonds, I became fascinated by the degree to which the selling qualities of shop floorspace could be affected quite materially by shop shapes and locations, by the proximity of such things as pedestrian crossings, bus stops and car parks, and fundamentally by ease and nature of pedestrian access. If I had known some of that a decade earlier I might have avoided the agonies of trying to let the Paternoster shops!

CHAPTER 10

Kensington and Elsewhere

IN 1968 TWO SENIOR urban partners retired and the remaining two, Jack Wix and my cousin Sam, thought that it was time for me to return from our City office to the head office in Westminster. By this time I had for some years past been an appointed Receiver to the Church Commissioners and Sam, who now took over as senior partner for the four years left before he too was due to retire, agreed that it was time for me to be appointed as a Receiver also to our second main client the Crown Estate. I was already well known to them, having been involved with Sam on a number of their cases but without, up to that point, dealing on a day to day basis with their Central London estates that were in our charge. My cousin, as I may have indicated already, was a complex character and the stories of his idiosyncrasies, both in and out of the office, were legion among the staff and his wide circle of acquaintances. A sometimes irascible bachelor, he could nevertheless be very kind to those in genuine need or trouble, while making no efforts to hide his impatience with those whose troubles were not so genuine. In the course of a very full life he had made himself an acknowledged authority in the worlds of horology, church and cathedral organ design and development and all forms of internal combustion engine, particularly the more vintage and veteran ones, some of which he used to race with some success and occasional, and spectacular, disaster. While he applied himself diligently to the business and to the office hours that some of his senior equals were inclined to prune a little, what he did during those hours was sometimes not much related to the work of the firm and he freely admitted that he only became a surveyor because, as in my case, he was told it was a family duty, and to finance his other interests.

The other partners in his age group, fearing that when he got into the driving seat things might be a little bizarre, as indeed in some respects they were, had some years earlier persuaded the partners to take business management largely out of the hands of the senior partner for the time being and to have the firm run by an appointed – later elected – management committee. As to his principal client responsibility, the Crown Estate official who was our main point of contact for the urban estates was at pains to urge me to take the reins from Sam sooner rather than later saying that, while he was an entertaining chap and one whom the Commissioners were always glad to have at their meetings, if they could not soon see a younger and more involved partner in charge of their work the firm was in danger of losing it. This proved to be far from easy as, although my cousin subscribed to the principle of handing over, he resisted most strongly in practice. This was despite my strenuous efforts to ease the transition in as many ways as I could. When he retired to the Isle of Man four years later his solicitor, who was a friend of mine, told me with some embarrassment that he had been instructed to cut me out of my cousin's will! Years later cordial relations were restored and at the end he was in fact generous both to me and to one of our sons, but it was a very hot seat for a while.

As I entered into the full stresses of senior partnership and responsibilities as appointed agent to most of our main urban clients, I was so fortunate to have such a happy and supportive family life at home in Sussex. Jill and I were both in our element with small children, and still are now with our grandchildren, and she was all that one could wish for as a mother and homemaker. However interesting the work of the day, the high point was always to catch the train home and the weekends did much to drain away the stresses of the week. Although I do not think that I am a particularly stressful person, there are aspects of trying to run a partnership that certainly do raise the blood pressure a bit, either through the occasional intransigence of partners or clients or when the figures, which were produced monthly by our internal accounting team, showed us nearing our overdraft limits. In the year that my parents both died, 1978, my mother said to me one evening 'You must get great satisfaction from being managing partner of Cluttons,' and was I think a little shocked when I answered, rather thoughtlessly, 'It's a bed of nails much of the time'. It must have been a bad day!

For the four years of his senior partnership Sam took over from Kenneth the appointment as Surveyor to the Trustees of Henry Smith's Charity for the extensive Kensington Estate that then constituted their principal asset. The work, for him, was not onerous because we had a local office on the Estate in the charge of a partner who ran the management team. Nevertheless, Sam announced his intention of taking the task seriously by starting each Tuesday with a meeting in the local office to discuss cases in hand. Most management cases, of letting, minor repairs and the like, are fairly routine and it was not long before the resident partner was finding difficulty in concocting an agenda that would cause Sam to do other than yawn. The problem was soon solved by my cousin getting into the habit, after an increasingly short business session, of 'popping off' as he put it, to the V and A, which was only a short distance away and which he found much more interesting.

When Sam retired in 1971 I had assumed that Leonard, who was responsible for other residential estates which I mainly was not, would be appointed in his place. The clients however made it pretty clear that they wanted another Clutton and so I took on this appointment, much to the relief of the partner in the

Family home at North Chailey from 1962 to 1995.

Kensington office as we had grown up in the firm together and he had found his four years answerable to my cousin to be something of a trial! This proved, over the next twenty years, to be a most enjoyable appointment, mainly because the Trust had no officer layer intervening between the Trustees and the agent, other than a treasurer and clerk who were partners in a firm of solicitors and to whom the Trust were also clients. I was therefore trusted to get on with the work, reporting regularly to the Estate Committee of the Trust and once a year to their full annual meeting. There was in fact quite a lot to do in addition to day to day management. The estate had come through the war in a run down condition, with a huge backlog of needed repairs and modernization, together with many vacant and dilapidated houses, including a substantial part that had been requisitioned. Houses that were unsuitable for conversion into flats therefore had to be let on long leases on condition that the lessees put them into repair. Those houses that were more suited to flat conversion were the subject of schemes originally by the Trustees themselves but, as the policy advanced and the programme was more than they could themselves finance, conversion blocks were let on building leases, with the developers in turn granting long leases to the occupiers of the new flats in return for improved ground rents and also capital premiums by which to recoup their outlay and pay in turn the Trustees' head lease premiums.

Considerable progress had been made on this situation before I came on the scene, but there was still much to do, particularly in arranging further building lettings for the conversion of still unimproved blocks of buildings. In consequence of the earlier works however, there were already at that time a very large number of residential long leaseholders of houses and flats on the Estate, each with leasehold interests of considerable value but, as the years went by, of ever shorter unexpired term. Landowners possessed of freehold residential estates let in this way had long been aware of the growing political risk that their assets could be taken away from them by statute on terms of artificially reduced value. Our Church and Crown clients had already largely divested themselves of these risky investments by offering residential freeholds to their lessees at prices that shared the considerable latent values inherent in these situations between lessor and lessee, on terms thus attractive to both.

It was apparent that the same risks existed in the case of the Kensington Estate which, in terms of numbers of leases, was also primarily residential. As an additional risk factor, the Estate comprised the main asset of the Trust, which thus had nearly all of its eggs in this one basket. Up to that point there had been a reluctance to sell freeholds from what was largely a ring fence estate, with the risk of creeping loss of control of amenity and management that had been maintained to a high standard via the covenants of the leases. We therefore prepared, in 1973, a major policy report the recommendation of which was that freeholds and control should be held but that all holders of long ground leases should be offered extensions of their leases, to put them in the position of being as nearly freeholders as was thought possible, in return for the payment of capital premiums that would realize to the Estate as much as possible of the latent value inherent from the ground lease situation. This latent value – or 'marriage' value as it is called – occurs when a ground lease term falls to an unexpired period of years that reduces value to the leaseholder, either because the limited tenure is unattractive to a purchaser or because it starts to become difficult to re-mortgage the property on sale, or both. Another factor is that the shorter the lease, the shorter the time for which a lessee may enjoy the benefits of his improvements; and in some of these houses the amounts spent on tenant's improvements were very considerable. The freehold interest value is also reduced in these circumstances, since the fixed ground rent is unattractive and the large eventual reversion value is heavily discounted, almost to vanishing point in circumstances of high interest rates.

This policy was accepted by the Trustees, both because realization of latent values would increase the overall value of their asset base and also because it would enable them to invest the proceeds of long lease sales in Stock Exchange securities and thus diversify from a potentially risky reliance upon property and, moreover, property confined to one location. Some lessees took up the offers; others waited until they wished to sell their leases when the availability of a lease extension both maximized the price and provided the cash with which to pay the new lease premium. This process proceeded for some years with great benefit to the Trust, until a new threat, applicable to both the long ground leases of houses and to shorter tenancies of houses and flats, emerged in the form of political pressures for leasehold enfranchizement. The Trustees took all means to protect their interests but the matter was brought to a head by an offer to purchase the whole freehold estate on terms that, after some negotiation, reflected the major part of remaining latent value. Several Trustees were glad of this opportunity as they understood the Stock Market rather better than they did property and it solved at a stroke their over reliance upon the Kensington Estate. Thus ended what to me had been a most rewarding appointment, with delightful clients and a real feeling that one's work and advice were making a difference in a situation in which everyone involved with the Estate, both tenants and landlords, benefited and there were really no losers. It was, to me at least, a bit of a wrench to sever relations with our oldest client, for whom my predecessors and I had acted for almost a quarter of a millennium, but I was glad to learn, after my retirement, that the firm continues to manage the Estate for the new owners.

I have concentrated upon the investment policy aspect of acting for this client, but an equally important part of our management duties was the preservation and conservation of an estate that consisted almost wholly of buildings, terraces and crescents listed as of architectural and historical interest. This dictated the need for high standards of management both for the owners and occupiers and also for the public at large who enjoyed the amenity values of the street facades, the squares and crescents and the sixteen gardens, large and small, around which the Estate was designed. Many building groups were stucco fronted, either as a whole or as to decorative courses, cornices and the like. The Estate reserved power in the leases to carry out regular repair and repainting of these building groups and to recover the cost from lessees in the proportional shares laid down in the leases. Not all lessees were happy with the disturbance of these repainting exercises and the nuisance of their homes being scaffolded during the warm weather time of the year that was best for this work, but most agreed that the effect was very attractive as a street scene, as well as being one that added value to their homes. To the surveyor team it was a hassle that was going on somewhere on the Estate each summer, but we all took pride in the results.

Towards the end of my term as Surveyor, when most of the flat conversions had been achieved, the Trustees responded positively to a recommendation to do something about the one remaining area of the Estate that had had little improvement, apart from replacement of the railings removed early in the war, namely the gardens. An expert was called in and over a period of four or five years every garden was rejuvenated to an agreed plan of new lawn layout, replanting of flower and shrub borders and re-routing and surfacing of paths. The fine stock of mature trees had always had expert attention but this work to the other aspects of these gardens was, to my mind at least, the final act in restoring one of London's most attractive Estates. It was far seeing of the Trustees to agree to it because the cost was significant and no definite return on the expenditure could be predicted. All agreed however that it could only enhance property values, to the benefit of freeholder and leaseholders alike.

Life was not all work and perhaps this account should not be either as, even in the thick of it in London, my thoughts were never far from home and our family. We were lucky to have an excellent prep school within ten minutes' drive which took children as day pupils for their first few terms until they and their parents were ready for the boarding environment that was there for most of the school company. The school was run by charming people, was fortunate in having very extensive grounds and gave, as time showed, a good education in happy circumstances. Our four sons went there in turn when they grew out of the pre-prep stage, while our daughter was a day pupil at Jill's former school in Burgess Hill. There, she arrived in the bottom form just as the school decided to raise its entry age by about three or four years. Thus, for that period she and her friends were always in the bottom form because the school removed the lowest level at the end of each year until their objective was achieved! The experience did Helen no harm and she had nearly fourteen happy years at the school before au-pairing in France and then attending Edinburgh University. The boys all went either to agricultural college, polytechnic or university, according to their choice and I was only glad that the firm produced the profits to make it all possible.

I have mentioned our Lakeland holidays when the children were small, when we stayed with our good friends at their house at Troutbeck, with ten small children between us and with trips out to the many valleys where we took turns either in baby minding or fell walking, interspersed with rustic picnics. These holidays were usually in October but as the children became committed to school terms, and also to relieve our hosts and give ourselves some variety, we hired houses in other parts of the District or ventured further afield with holiday houses and hotels in Ireland, Cornwall, Scotland and elsewhere; trying to interest our family in as much of the beauty of their native islands as possible. From their own inclination to take their own families to the same scenery I like to think that we succeeded. We did try a few journeys to Central Europe, as well as to the Channel Islands, not always with the whole family but at least with the younger ones, and they also made individual journeys in school groups that helped to expand their horizons. However, we really preferred home territory, supplemented by a swimming pool in the garden and over four hundred acres of Common outside the garden gate, that solved much of the problem of keeping active

*One of the late William IV and early Victorian crescents on the former
Kensington Estate of Henry Smith's Charity. Photograph by Niall Clutton.*

children amused during the long summer holidays. When the family had grown up we found the logistics of just the two of us visiting more distant places much easier and we have been lucky enough to see quite a bit of the world, leaving our adult family to arrange their own more venturesome holidays abroad with their children, which they do.

My attempts to sail as a hobby were intermittent. The dinghy that I built from a kit was parked on the part of the shingle beach allotted to the Brighton Sailing Club. There was no shortage of fellow members who, lacking a boat of their own, were glad to form a crew. Races started between the piers and a popular course took us round a marker buoy off Shoreham harbour. The dinghy hull was constructed with built-in buoyancy tanks and was therefore unsinkable despite filling with a fair bit of ocean on a windward run. As a solution, I fitted self bailers in the hull – with some trepidation as one does not lightly bore holes into the bottom of a boat! When planing with the wind astern these worked splendidly, emptying the boat in a matter of minutes with the sound of a bath waste. These races were exhilarating sailing, so long as you remembered to close the self bailers when slowing down! I sold the boat when our second baby arrived because I did not really like to absent myself at weekends. I ought to have kept it. The sail number was fifty and there are now thousands of them. Perhaps I should advertise 'come in number fifty, your time is up' and see if the only example of my boat building era may still be sitting on a beach somewhere. The next two boats, a Gypsy and a Twister, were moored at Newhaven and I and friends had many a weekend sail that we usually enjoyed, but there was always the inevitable crewing guest who delighted in telling his experiences of spending the whole of a Saturday outing shrouded in thick fog and wishing he were elsewhere, if only he knew in what direction elsewhere might lie.

The family never really took to sailing and Jill did definitely not like to be in open water in a small boat! So, when property market doldrums hit, the boats tended to go. I had one last go in 1978, with a Golden Hind motor sailor moored at the new Brighton Marina. That boat was in regular use for several years, but with seldom long enough away to get much beyond the Solent and round the Isle of Wight. I finally sold for the last time to a man from Fort William who took the boat out of the Marina one late winter morning with a friend to help him, with the intention of sailing home up the North Sea and through the Caledonian Canal. Before leaving, and obviously not thinking much of my lifeline attachments, he put two large ring bolts into the sides of the cockpit well, where there was already not overmuch room for the legs. When he left I watched the weather forecasts for some days. The winds were mostly north easterly and I wondered how he, and particularly his shins, were faring. By far my longest sail was long ago in 1951 with a fellow member of the Royal Thames Yacht Club who had had his coal mine nationalized and had spent the proceeds on a large schooner that he wished to bring down from the Holy Loch to the Hamble. I had an exciting week's crewing, not without a few alarms and excursions, including a very near miss of grounding on the Arklow Bank in the Irish Sea. When I dived into Dunloaghaire harbour, which was unexpectedly and freezingly cold, I was roundly ticked off by my host for dripping salt water on to the saloon carpet. A few nights later we came through the Longships Channel off Lands End in the height of the storm that caused the Lynmouth disaster and the whole of the carpet was, for a time, under water. I felt that honour was satisfied.

Two different forms of Customs clearance impressed me on that holiday. The boat arrived in Ireland flying the yellow jack to indicate that it had come from a foreign port and some hours later a gentleman in a rowing boat came alongside and handed up a clearance form, already completed to say that there was nothing to declare, and asked someone to sign it; which someone did and he rowed off again. A few days later we arrived in Falmouth in raging seas and violent winds, again flying the yellow flag, and only just able to make it to a mooring in the Roads in atrocious conditions. These however did not deter the local Customs, who were alongside in a launch almost before we were secured and who insisted on making a thorough inspection despite the still lively movement of the boat. I certainly felt back in England.

CHAPTER 11

The Crown Estate

I WAS AN APPOINTED Receiver to the Crown Estate for exactly a quarter of a century, from 1968 until 1993, and it was a great privilege to act for such a client and to be responsible for such interesting estates. These were mainly in St James's and other parts of central Westminster, but including also some outlying holdings and with occasional requests to advise on situations further afield. I was only able to hold this appointment, in addition to a similar one for the Church Commissioners and the subsequent one for Smith's Charity, because I had such excellent partners to carry out much of the actual management work. This however was not initially the case with the Crown Estate. At about the time that I took over, the principal management assistant left to advance his career elsewhere, anticipating that there might not be room for a second partner for that particular work. In fact, while he may well have judged correctly at the time, the work was soon to expand, making the need for a second person of partner status to work with me essential. That, though, was still a little way off and for the present I found myself at the opposite extreme of having almost no assistance at all above the very junior level. For a time I had a succession of short lived but inadequate more senior assistants. During that period, which I suppose lasted about a year, I had to do a great deal of the day to day work myself, until one of the other management partners was able to spare time to help out. It was a great day for me when, later on, I was able to recruit an assistant of the same abilities as those who helped me with the other major clients and who soon became, like them, a very valued partner.

The estates in our charge were still recovering from the effects of war, mainly because they contained a high proportion of large and important buildings – many later to be Grade One or Two listed – where the problems and costs of restoration were major ones that much of the market avoided in favour of opportunities that were less challenging, or capable of producing more predictable investment rewards at that time. When I came on the scene there were still several vacant buildings, many others that were being used at far below their value potential and sites to be brought back into appropriate use, as well as occupied buildings where the leaseholders had to be persuaded, by the grant of suitable new leases, to modernize the buildings themselves. One of the most conspicuous of the largely unoccupied groups of buildings was Carlton House Terrace in the Mall. While a few houses in these terraces, notably those of the Royal Society and Crockfords, were occupied, most were not, or contained only temporary tenants making use of inexpensive floor space. Moreover, several had had water entering through un-repaired roofs and walls, with the result that dry and wet rot were widespread. In fact, conditions were so bad that at one time the Crown Estate Commissioners had been advised by independent consultants to demolish these Nash terraces entirely and to make the site available for redevelopment. To the rear, one large site was still a wartime emergency water supply tank and, of course, all of the front area railings had, as elsewhere, been cut off early in the war to provide iron for munitions and armament construction. One of the few opportunities for a laugh in those early days came when we found that these railings had all been stacked in the basement of one of the houses. So much for the war effort!

The main timber floors were double; that is, with one set of massive joists supporting the floor and another set holding the ceiling beneath, with a gap between the two. Also the original builders, when the brick walls were first raised, omitted to remove the timber stays that were fixed to provide temporary support to the window frames prior to the walls being built up between each frame. Thus rot in the floor timbers could only be dealt with by major and expensive surgery and dry rot developing in one window frame could, and did, travel along the stays encased within the brickwork until many of the windows were affected and the spores could be almost anywhere within the substantial brick walls. These buildings presented a daunting and expensive problem, particularly as they could not, because of their historical associations, prominent location, and unusual internal design and decorative standards, be let for their potentially most valuable use as commercial offices.

Slowly however tenants were found, of an 'institutional' character acceptable to the planning authority in that location. Architects drew up schemes for repair and restoration acceptable to the Commissioners and their Historic Buildings Adviser and these, as can be seen by visitors to the premises today, were imaginative and such as generally to do justice to the potential and character of Nash's original concept, with decorative features copied from archive photographs and rare fireplaces, etc., recovered from storage wherever they could be found. The Commissioners themselves occupied three, and later four, houses and the podiums fronting the Mall were converted for use as car parking and art galleries. Our job was to arrange building leases and prepare the structures for the restorations to come, either by employing contractors to eradicate dry rot or by supervising very closely the lessees' works to ensure that any more rot uncovered as they proceeded was adequately removed. The next task, once there were lessees to contribute to the cost through the lease service charges, was to arrange the first comprehensive post-war repair of the stucco rendering to the facades, followed by the first painting for many a year. In the event, when the stucco was hammer tapped all over its surface, much of it was discovered to be un-keyed and we had to have it replaced with the best match that could be achieved to the original.

I have described what was done to these buildings because, although they were perhaps the extreme case, the same sort of thing had to be achieved in many other situations where buildings were of architectural or historic significance and therefore had to be preserved if at all possible. Elsewhere, in a few cases where the buildings were historic but too far gone to be kept, developers were found to rebuild. By this means the estates gained some distinctive new buildings, such as the Economist Building and New Zealand House, before my time, and the Intercontinental Hotel, plus other rebuilds or major reconstructions in the original style and character, such as Hobhouse Court off Suffolk Street and the Coutts Bank headquarters in the Strand. It was a busy and exciting time and one had the feeling that our work was making a very positive contribution, with that of many others, to the Nation's heritage in that part of London. One of these largely new buildings was the Charing Cross Police Station, built on the site of the former hospital off the Strand. Inspecting this on behalf of the Estate shortly before its completion gave me what I hope was to be my sole experience of the inside of a cell. It was a chilling sight, and these ones were brand new!

On these estates, as for much of the Church estates following pre-war emphasis on security of income and avoidance of risk, there were still a great many buildings outstanding on long lease at fixed ground rents. When we and the surveyors for the other large Crown estate in Regent Street were asked to assess the reversionary potential of the holdings the income graph rose slowly but steadily until the early years of the twenty first century. It then took off nearly vertically as long leases were due to run out and the Commissioners would revert to the occupational rack rents. As the revenue from the Estate is paid to the Treasury this situation was thought to be politically unacceptable. There was a risk that the Government of the moment, with short term financial imperatives, might press the Commissioners to sell the Estate, or at least these parts of it, so that capital receipts reflecting this reversionary potential could be reinvested to produce a considerable and immediate increase in revenue to the Exchequer. I have tried to explain, in the case of Smith's Charity, the latent value inherent in these ground lease situations; far greater for these large commercial buildings than for individual houses in Kensington and with that latent element being greater still where the site had potential for improvement or development of the kind that could only be financed by a longer lease term. There was thus further value to be achieved for the Estate by granting leases long enough to allow lessees, as a condition of the grant, to improve or, in appropriate cases, to redevelop, so as to enhance the rental potential in which both the freeholder and the leaseholder would then participate in agreed shares and in improved, reviewable, terms. Value considerations apart, these policies also enabled the Commissioners to fulfil what they considered to be another important obligation of their stewardship; the restoration, improvement and modernisation of the properties in their charge.

In addition to our normal duties of management we were therefore instructed to seek opportunities for renegotiation of leases where these advantages could be obtained, which would go some way to smoothing the rental projections. I and my colleagues were engaged on this work for most of my time as a Receiver. I lost count of the number of leasehold situations thus

Cluttons' Equity partners in 1982. I am centre of the front row, my brother Nigel to my left and my senior partner predecessor Peter Trumper to my right. My successor Richard Jonas, from 1992 to 2003, standing fifth from left and his successor as senior partner, Richard Cotton between Peter and me in the back row.

unscrambled – some of them twice in the course of the twenty five years – but at a tally late in my career the number had exceeded the hundred mark. Some of these negotiations took years to achieve results. One such was a former large hotel in Buckingham Gate which, with the rest of the island street block, eventually, after about twenty years of talking and planning, became the Government offices that exist today.

The longest case by far was the redevelopment of the 'Criterion' block bounded by Piccadilly Circus, Lower Regent Street, Jermyn Street and the Haymarket. There had already been fifteen years of planning and negotiations with the lease owners on the site, principally Fortes and London Transport, the latter being also concerned about the effect of building foundations on their station and tube lines, before I came on the scene. It took nearly all of my tenure to achieve the buildings that now stand on this prominent site – a total gestation of some forty years! It is a convention to give design schemes an identify-ing letter and to take the next one in the alphabet when a scheme has to be substantially modified or replaced by a new one. The Criterion development was the only one in my busy life of either arranging or being concerned with new building projects that went right through the alphabet. As I recollect, the scheme that was eventually built was letter 'C' the second time around.

This work was a far cry from my first experience of helping, as the most junior of the team, to manage Crown property when I started work in 1949, some of which I have tried to describe, including my first and failed task over the matter of the pavement lights. When I worked for Drivers Jonas there were still many pavement lights with holes in them where the glass lozenges had broken. Some gentlemen of the road were quick on the uptake and I think we were paying out either five or ten shillings to anyone coming to the office with a limp that they claimed they had incurred by an ankle twist in one of our buildings' broken pavement lights.

When we were closing streets for comprehensive development schemes in the City one had to apply for a Street Closing Order, the applications being published in the usual way. An enterprising gentleman living somewhere in North London did quite well out of watching for these applications and then coming to state that he had grounds for objection as he had been in the habit of walking along the street for most of his life. The authorities had to take claims of prescriptive rights seriously. Even if they were spurious, as they probably were, there could be expensive delays if the matter had to be thrashed out through the formal procedures. It was better to find the price at which the objection would be withdrawn. Another source of development delay could be the finding of ancient artefacts on a site. A period was usually allowed for these to be investigated but the delay could be very expensive for the developer. In conversation with one such many years ago, he told me of an ancient sarcophagus discovered entombed in the basements of buildings being cleared for development, complete with effigy of a knight in armour on top. 'Gracious!' I said. 'What did you do with it?' thinking of it in some museum. 'Walled it up quick!' was the answer, so presumably it is still there.

Not all Crown properties were of the grander sort. As the junior in the office in those early days I was sent down to the reception hall one afternoon because a Crown tenant in Soho had come in to complain about something. When I got there the usual reception staff were nowhere in evidence but there was a little old lady sitting on a chair in the most appalling stench. I cannot now remember the nature of the complaint or how I dealt with it but the experience was such that, half a century later when many names have vanished from my memory, I can still recall hers as if it were yesterday.

Most of the St James's clubs are on the Crown Estate. At a time in the seventies when clubs generally were finding the financial going difficult, the Commissioners were worried that they might find themselves with vacant club houses on their hands that were both difficult to let and expensive listed buildings to maintain. I therefore had to do a survey of each one and report upon the condition and letability of the buildings. Given that the Planning Authority was not willing to allow open commercial use and that the buildings were mostly purpose built in any case, I found it difficult to suggest alternative occupants in the market conditions of that time and had to confirm that there could indeed be a problem if any of these leases should fall in. Subsequently, an increase in demand for top quality premises for gaming would have been the solution in some cases but this was less so in the seventies and the then Commissioners did not want, in any case, to encourage this activity on their estates. The answer was therefore to persuade the clubs of the benefits to their futures in taking new and longer leases, conditionally upon their making agreed repairs and improvements. To save the clubs being saddled with significant rental outgoings, the consideration for these new leases was taken largely as capital premiums. The premium in one case was generously paid in its entirety by one member. In another, a club was able to pay its premium from the proceeds of sale of a valuable bust found in the attic. I was told that this led to some intensive searching of attics elsewhere!

A fresh blow fell to clubs in these old buildings when the local authority employed a public health inspector who decided to throw the book at some of them. One of the club secretaries 'phoned me to let me know that he would have to seek the freeholder's consent for some of the resultant works. He went on to say that the club had been served with a schedule of a large number of defects to be remedied. Some of these he accepted were fair comment but he took particular exception to an

The Quadrega of Helios fountain on the new Criterion Development on the Crown Estate. Photograph by Niall Clutton.

accusation of rising damp in the wine cellars, saying that in his experience this had been a feature of all the best wine cellars that he had known and that he had been rather proud of it. The values involved in helping these clubs to survive were not large in the context of estate values as a whole, but the club uses are important to the particular mix of building uses that make the St James's London scene so unique. I was therefore glad that the Commissioners took the enlightened view over new leases that they did. This certainly helped one or two clubs to survive that might otherwise well have gone under, and it was nice to be a part of the efforts to secure their futures.

Having first worked with Crown Estate properties in 1949, I finished doing so forty five years later. My involvement was not continuous but this client was never far away and I often helped my seniors with cases while being otherwise engaged elsewhere.

This kept me in touch with the Commissioners' staff and some of them became good friends, although always with the slight distance that has to separate principal and agent. The Estate was a good client to the firm; as it still is. I recall only one embarrassing hiccup. This occurred when we first computerized our collection of rents. Most clients paid commission in arrears; either monthly or quarterly, but the Crown Estate at that time paid in advance. The computer was instructed accordingly but was not told to omit collection in arrears and happily took commission both at the beginning and the end of each period. It was nearly eighteen months later that the error, which had not been picked up by either our or the client's auditors, was spotted by one of our rental clerks. The overpayments, which by then were not insignificant, were refunded immediately, with interest, and we stopped wondering vaguely why we seemed to be doing better than our income budgets had predicted.

The Commissioners were not necessarily grand people. Our driver took me to a Crown Estate meeting in Carlton House Terrace one morning and said as we approached 'Look at that Sir. Isn't it disgraceful that someone should chain that tatty old bike to the railings.' I had to tell him that the conveyance in question belonged to the noble lord who was the current First Commissioner.

At the end of my long involvement someone kindly recommended me for a modest gong. Standing beside Her Majesty, the Lord Chamberlain said 'For services to the Crown Estate' which prompted the Queen to ask me how long I had been with the Estate. This foxed me and, feeling that I could not possibly explain in the few seconds permitted what my actual connection with the Estate had been, I muttered something pretty incoherent, expressed my thanks, and withdrew. I like to hope that she was used to people being bundles of nerves, rather than thinking me a complete idiot.

CHAPTER 12

Valuation

MY LIFE AND WORK at Cluttons so far described has been largely to do with the firm's basic work which, at that time and still to a large extent today, has been the management of large landed estates; in my case, urban estates. Thus the clients could reasonably expect to receive the revenues properly due to them and to be relieved of most of the management chores. They could also expect their agents to watch for ways in which to improve the nature of their holdings, by improvement of leasing structures and by development and improvement of the actual bricks and mortar, either by investing further in the properties themselves or by allowing others to do so on terms whereby they as landlords received some of the latent values thus released. The one thing about their property assets of which they were largely ignorant, however, was what they were worth. The best that could be done was to apply a capitalization multiplier to each class of rental revenue to give an approximate indication of aggregate value, so that some estimation could be made of the relative proportions of the overall portfolio that were attributable to property and to stocks and shares and, within the property part, to urban as against rural holdings.

When I first started work our major clients thought that this was as far as they could reasonably go. There was no great perceived need to know more accurately the value of their holdings and the costs of obtaining this information on any regular basis were thought to be considerable and unjustified. With their principal liabilities being for income distribution to religious or charitable beneficiaries – or in the case of the Crown Estate to the Exchequer – it was this income, rather than its capital value, in which such clients were mainly interested.

At that time Cluttons had no specialist valuation department on either the urban or rural sides. Clients did of course need property valuations from time to time and these were done by those partners who felt able to take them on; i.e. those with at least some familiarity with the property markets and knowledge, or the ability to obtain it, of relevant market evidence. I have mentioned the shop valuations on which, as a junior, I assisted my then senior partner Jack Wix. A few years later the same client requested a valuation of a much larger chain of shops throughout England, and another in Northern Ireland. Another client sent Leonard Simkins and me to value a large department store in Newcastle on Tyne, at about the same time that other partners were busy with valuation of the whole of the Bedford Estates following the death of the then Duke. A little later on we were instructed on a major case involving the whole of Letchworth Garden City. These are examples of the kinds of instruction that varied the bread and butter estate management. There were many smaller cases.

Sam was instructed as expert witness for the owners of Letchworth but he relied on one of his younger partners to do most of the property inspections and the valuations. This meant that there were times when he was less au fait with his subject than perhaps he should have been, although he was seldom at a loss for words in such circumstances. Opposing Counsel; 'Mr Clutton. You have valued number twenty four in this street at the figure in your evidence but on the next page the value of number twenty five, an exactly similar property in every respect, appears at twice as much. Is there an explanation of that?' Mr Clutton; 'Yes. I must have been off my head.'

An interesting case that fell to me concerned the Portman

Estate lying to the north of Oxford Street. The Estate was to be divided in its ownership so that, while it would continue to be managed as one holding, each beneficiary of the Trust would have an agreed group of properties identified as his or her share; the allocated groups being determined according to the nature and age of each beneficiary and their priorities for income either immediately or at some future date. The valuations were made by the firm of the Estate Surveyor but an independent certification that these were reasonably and correctly made was required by the representatives of the various beneficiaries. I was instructed to carry out this task during a very cold winter in the early seventies. Armed with the information and estate terriers supplied to us by the Surveyor, my assistant and I inspected as many properties as we could in the time allowed, and as seemed to us to be reasonably representative of the several types of building, occupation and forms of letting on the Estate. We then walked up and down the numerous streets, mews and squares, taking notes of building type and condition and relevant details of location; particularly retail location. It was bitterly cold and about two hours of note taking was our limit before we had to find a cafe in which to thaw our hands before sallying forth again with our note books. Eventually the job was done and there came a day when we were asked to attend at the High Court where the ownership reallocations were to be ratified – presumably in case any last minute questions should come up that we might be able to answer. When we got there the courtroom seating was entirely occupied by be-wigged barristers, one at least for each beneficiary, and surveyors and even solicitors had to kick their heels in the corridor. Nevertheless, it is fun to be able to say that one once valued a hundred acres of Central London in a week. Not quite true of course, because someone else had done the donkey work and our task was primarily to check it.

*View from our Great College Street conference suite at night. Busts of my
Great Grandfather John (right) and my Grandfather John Henry.
Photograph by Niall Clutton.*

These are examples of the kinds of valuation instructions that
were done for largely non-management clients on demand.
There were many cases undertaken by one partner or another
but, at that time, none that had to be repeated on a regular basis.
I think the first request for regular and frequent valuation was
my appointment as independent valuer to the newly set up Save
and Prosper Property Bond; one of a number of similar property
unit investment vehicles started in the early seventies. This
required inspection of all of the Fund Manager's acquisitions on
purchase and subsequently at least once a year, or more
frequently if the valuer considered it necessary. The valuations
then had to be revised, to reflect the passage of time or any
detectable changes of value indicated by transaction evidence;

originally monthly but afterwards every fortnight, to coincide with updating of the unit prices quoted in the market for buying and selling.

To start with, the task was repetitive but not too difficult. There were only a few properties and I used to take a suitcase of files home at the weekend and work through the calculations in the peace of our dining room on a Sunday afternoon. When, after a year or two, the units started to attract buyers in large numbers however, the job became rather more difficult. It was at about this time that we completed the long and complicated task of computerizing all of our rental collections, payment of client's outgoings, etc., using at the time a firm of software advisers and contracting time on a main frame computer situated somewhere in Kent. Only later on were we able to take advantage of the rapid advances in this technology and have our own computers in house. I consulted with our receivership department head, who had learned to be something of a computer boffin himself, and he agreed that it should be possible to write the software necessary to replicate the property valuation tables and to apply them to the usual valuation data.

One morning therefore I armed myself with valuation tables, which include the formulae whereby each of them are calculated, locked my office door, put a metaphorical wet towel round my head, and carefully wrote out the data input fields and the formulae to make use of them for freehold and leasehold valuations respectively, with instructions to the software expert as to how the calculations were to be made and the sequence in which they were to be applied. At about midday I emerged to my secretary; job finished and calling for coffee! The programmes were fairly basic, but they did the main job, with fields for inserting capital additions or deductions as a means for dealing with any complications and with built in allowance for such things as purchaser's costs. Floor areas could be put in by floors or shop zones, to allow different rental prices to be applied to each, and the years' purchase date and time fields allowed the calculations automatically to reflect change in elapsed time – to lease reversion or rent review dates for instance – of a month or so; i.e., at least as sensitively as a purchaser would value in practice. I was delighted when the test runs worked, as was the Fund Manager when he saw it all, although he did give me a jolt a short time afterwards by ringing to say that our computer could not add – only to 'phone apologetically a little later to say that it was they who could not add and not us! At last I no longer had to take files home and the computer was thereafter run automatically at the prescribed intervals, with my involvement in the arithmetic being limited to passing through any new or varied information to be incorporated prior to each run.

I only ever knowingly met a holder of Save and Prosper property bonds once. This happened when I was inspecting a large warehouse on an industrial estate. One of the fork lift truck drivers, watching me using the measuring tape, became curious and asked me the purpose of my work, which I explained to him, naming the client as there was no secrecy in the case. 'Oh,' he said, 'I've got some of those. I'm not sure I would have bought them if I had known that they were invested in rubbish like this.' He was a bit hard. It was a brand new unit and quite a good investment as it turned out. I suppose he had thought that these investments were confined to shiny office blocks.

Today such a simple valuation programme sounds child's play but at the time I felt quite pleased with it. In fact, I did not realize just how useful this application of the computer was soon to be. The property bonds were a new addition to the various investors in property, notably the property companies themselves and the managed funds that the institutions were creating to meet demands for pension premium investment, that had to value their assets regularly to give validity to the share or unit prices. This information was then available to analysts and others to compare investment performance as between one investment vehicle and another, as well as enabling the funds to use a good performance record for advertising purposes.

This growing emphasis upon performance measurement and an ability to quote asset values with some reliability in annual reports was not lost upon the secretariat at the Church Commissioners but they were still concerned about justifying valuation costs. We were not the only agents serving them who had now devised simple computer programmes for repetitive commercial property valuations. Together with representatives of the other main receiver firms I therefore attended a meeting to examine how we might reach the point at which reliable performance measurement statistics could be made available. The Commissioners were not a body selling investment units on the market and it was agreed therefore that it was not essential, given the cost implications, for valuations to be prepared by firms independent of property management or any other service to the Commissioners. The retained managing agents, it was assumed, had all the necessary data to hand and should be able to do the job at a much smaller cost. It was therefore agreed that each agent should value the properties in his firm's management so that the Commissioners could use this information in their next Annual Report and, after a few years of repeat valuations, be able to start making report statements as to the investment performance of their property assets. The report would make it clear that the values were based upon the opinions of the managing agents, as was thought to be adequate in the circumstances.

Within Cluttons, properties under management comprised commercial, residential and agricultural holdings. The latter two categories did not at the time fit the simple computer programmes, but the number of residential properties in our charge for this client was not large at the time and the agricultural holdings, although large in terms of aggregate acreage, as a farm count were also such that the mechanics of valuation were not all that difficult. The main problem, despite the computer aid, was with the still large number of commercial lettings, plus several development schemes in progress. The latter had to be valued individually each time. When we came to input commercial property data we realized just how much of this was lacking on our files, due either to many years having passed since the last rental negotiations or to the fact that the manager's records of floor areas had no doubt been intelligible to him but were rather less so to his successors. Several of us therefore had to sandwich in with our other work a lot of referencing inspections on the ground and a search of property files for reliable plans, where they existed, from which to extract the missing measurements in the office. With the cut off date looming for production of the Annual Report, the first valuation was a little approximate in parts but in subsequent years the uncertainties in the data were steadily made good. The discipline of knowing that reliable data was needed for each property, whether or not it was otherwise 'active', meant that no inspection opportunity was missed for re-checking floorspace and other relevant facts.

The Crown Estate, being very conscious of control of management costs deducted from the annual revenue transfers to the Exchequer, took longer to be persuaded of the desirability of being able to put a value on the Estate assets and to monitor investment performance. When the Commissioners did decide to proceed we had a major referencing task as there were many ground lettings where there had been no occasion to measure the buildings for many years and where therefore our files were virtually empty. Fortunately, lessees' original development drawings were mostly on record, either in our files or those of the client, and our files contained full records of all consents under the leases for alterations and improvements, together with the drawings of what had been done. Some of the drawings were old and many were missing, so a good bit of re-referencing had to be done by inspection. Finding reasons to reinspect our clients' buildings from time to time, to check on condition and maintenance by lessees, was part of the management process so this need for referencing was not altogether an extra task. However, I do remember many long summer evenings in the office when, after finishing the more pressing jobs of the day, I would settle down to scaling rolls of plans, with a target of recording the floor areas of two more of the large St James's office blocks before leaving for home.

My other main client, the Trustees of Henry Smith's Charity, at that time made no annual report, other than to the Charity Commission, and had no need for regular property valuation. This was fortuitous as the Kensington Estate comprised many hundreds of houses and flats, in all conditions of leasing, and valuation would have been a major exercise that would have had to be carried out largely property by property and without the benefit of the computer. We did, nevertheless, make approximate valuations by broad bands of property category, with some 'informed' estimates of average reversionary rental values, in order periodically to be able to advise the Trustees as to how their estate was performing as an investment. In my last two years, when as a Consultant I was not too hard pressed, I attempted a more detailed valuation by reference to the comprehensive property data that we kept on card index and relying on my younger partner in charge of the management for average rental or reversionary capital values for each property or property block, plus advice on investment yields of the specialist

Valuation Department that the firm had by then established. This enabled me to give the Trustees a report upon performance over my twenty-plus years of stewardship and it was also helpful, I hope, to my successor who almost immediately had to guide the Trustees through negotiations on an offer, subsequently agreed, to sell the whole Estate.

The decision by the Crown Estate to have annual valuations of their properties roughly coincided, as far as I recall, with a movement to establish a National index against which the performance of such holdings could be measured. The idea, which was the brainchild of Rupert Nabarro and Ian Cullen and which subsequently came into being as the Investment Property Data Bank, was sponsored by a group of the leading London firms and was based upon an index of agricultural investment values that Rupert had pioneered for those of the group with major land agency and investment businesses.

The idea depended upon the establishment of a data bank sufficiently large to be representative of the property market, and activity within it, as a whole. It thus depended upon participation by as many as possible of the major insurance and other institutions and also by significant owners of commercial property estates throughout the land if it was to constitute a reliable benchmark of the Nation's property holdings, of investment and disinvestment and of the performance of rents and prices. To gain the support needed the process had to be wholly confidential and the data input in such a way that no individual holdings or their ownership could be identifiable. It was hard going initially to convince these bodies firstly that they would benefit from such a service and secondly that it could be achieved with the total security from identification of their individual circumstances that they were entitled to expect. It was a great credit to Rupert and his small team that the necessary cooperation was secured and I was pleased that, without of course any prompting from me as a director, the Chief Surveyor to the Legal and General Group brought the Group's data in as one of the first of the major property holding institutions to give their support.

It somehow fell to me to coordinate the sponsoring firms and to keep them all on board during the start up phase. This was no easy task at times as sponsorship funds were needed from us all to get things going and not all partners in a few of these firms agreed with this use of their money. Eventually however the enterprise took off and it is now well established in its production of performance reports covering all aspects of this for each category of commercial property, region by region throughout the country. The Crown Estate Commissioners, particularly, were gratified to have the valuation data of their own holdings that enabled them to point, in their Annual Reports, to the highly favourable performance of the Estate when measured against this National index.

For my part, I have always found the art of valuation a fascinating one and I was lucky to be entrusted with so much of it. Sometimes there was rather too much of it of a similar and tedious nature, such as the exercise in Brixton in the sixties, but shop inspections, and the evaluation of different parts and parades within any one town centre, were a constant source of interest and challenge. I also enjoyed the occasional escape from the pressures of the office and would book my car on Motorail to Aberdeen or Inverness, my northernmost points of call, and work my way back through the week, making inspections as I went. When these were for valuation no secrecy was required and I waved a letter of authority to inspect at the shop manager on my arrival. If one were inspecting, on behalf of a prospective purchaser, a property that was for sale, the vendors often did not want the shop manager to know what might be afoot until a sale should be achieved. Prospective purchaser's surveyors would then have to play it by ear. On being asked the purpose of inspection on one such occasion I said something like 'Routine insurance check.' 'That's funny,' said the shop manager, 'yours is the fourth insurance check this week.'

Some managers checked one's credentials with care. Jack and I once travelled to Bridport by train. I remember the occasion particularly because we had to change to the local flyer at a place called Maiden Newton and the station master was so surprised at having first class passengers on his hands that he had to fetch a special key with which to unlock the one such compartment that the train contained; beautifully upholstered and smelling strongly of mothballs. The shop to be inspected had closed for lunch, which gave us time to look at the shopping generally and to evaluate the position of the shop to be valued. When it at last reopened, our turn round at Bridport had to be fairly quick in order to catch one of the few return trains. While the shop manager was phoning his head office to check that our letter of introduction was authentic, we quickly ran the measuring rod over the floor space. When the manager returned to say that we could proceed he was a little taken aback by Jack saying, as we left for the train, 'That's all right thank you. We have seen all that we want.'

Today, work of this sort is done by a specialist department. In this context, as in many others, I have often felt glad to have come in to the profession during a period when one was expected to be something of an all rounder. If life was more challenging it was also much more interesting. The Save and Prosper Property Manager, I know, regularly checked my valuations out with his buying agents and he was kind enough to tell me that there was seldom any serious difference. I liked to think that sometimes being a jack of all trades did not necessarily imply mastership of none.

CHAPTER 13

Diversions

MY WORK AS A senior partner in the firm did not end with my three main clients, or indeed with other clients. I was lucky to enjoy more diversity in my professional life than fell to most of my partners. Jack Wix succeeded Sam as the firm's senior partner in 1972. I have recorded how, as a junior, I toured the country with him valuing shops and that he was principally the partner who introduced me to the partnership at such an early age. By the time that he took the chair he regarded me as perhaps his closest confidante and discussed with me the many problems that he faced, for which we then worked out the best answers to put to the partnership. He had spent four war years in Germany after being captured in the Western Desert and it may have been this experience that contributed to the heavy smoking that, in the end, probably led to his premature death in 1979 at the age of no more than sixty eight. After a severe heart attack when he was in his mid fifties his hours in the office were thereafter shortened but he still looked after one important client and he chaired the firm's Management Committee which by this time exercised most of the functions of running the business. He was interested in this and he had a flair for getting on with everyone, by whom he was well liked, and for spotting and defusing potential trouble spots. He brought in an accountancy firm that did wonders for our tax planning and he also recruited our first internal administrator who taught us how to budget and to run systems that helped us to know what work earned profits and what did not. He had four years as senior partner before retiring but by his half way point, in about 1974, he was not a well man and, finding it all very taxing, handed over the effective job of managing partner to me. I was therefore chairing the business management of the firm for eight years before taking over as senior partner from my agricultural equivalent senior, Peter Trumper, followed by the ten years during which I was then, in turn, the firm's senior partner. As with my professional work, I could not have covered the ground without the help of very expert colleagues and I did not normally have to get tied down too closely in the nitty gritty of administration when there were staff much more capable than myself who only needed a steer or a decision from time to time.

A potential problem in any partnership is that partners can be tempted to under-charge their own clients, knowing that most individual fees are only a very small part of the firm's income when taken in isolation. This weakness was brought to our attention by a partner who was a little taken aback by his senior, Sam, who, receiving a complaint from the client that a fee was too high, wrote in reply offering to toss a coin with him for it, double or quits! One of the tasks of administration was therefore to monitor fee quotes, particularly after the customary scales had been withdrawn, to ensure that the firm received the fees to which it was properly entitled. Another was to deal with the tricky and sensitive matter of office cars, to which all partners and a number of senior staff were entitled. It was said of some people that one might get away with reducing their salary, or at least not increasing it, in times of difficulty, but if their class of car were downgraded there would be trouble. We heard that in other firms the full partnership would often waste a great deal of time arguing about cars, desks, etcetera and we made strenuous efforts to avoid doing the same by ensuring that, when these matters had to be thrashed out, only a minimum number of us would be deflected from income earning in order to do it. Not all efforts to ensure payment of fees were successful. Jack submitted what he thought was a modest fee account to a lady client only to receive a letter in reply, addressed to the firm rather than to him individually, saying 'Mr Wix is a very charming man, but it takes more than charm to make me write a cheque.' He thought the back handed compliment at least worth the small fee and let it rest.

Administrators did a good and essential job but, by their nature, they did not appear in the departmental accounts as direct fee earners. Cluttons had been one of the first of the major firms to computerize rental collections and it was a great day when the Crown Estate put the whole of their collection of rents on all of their estates out to tender and the firm won the contract. We probably did so because the Government's own computer services, with whom we were in competition, were not fully geared to this slightly specialized operation. In due course the job was taken back by them but for the best part of a decade I was very glad for our administrative teams who were able to have a major client and an income flow to their direct credit.

Apart from the diversion of playing a part in the running of the firm, as opposed to the direct service of its clients, I was frequently instructed on interesting one-off cases. Some of these were arbitrations, although the contestants often had a distressing tendency to settle as soon as I was appointed! One that was not settled in advance was a rental dispute between London Transport, who owned Shepherd's Bush Market, and the large number of shop tenants whose leases were up for renewal. We held the arbitration in my firm's conference suite, the biggest room that we had available. A large number of tenants decided to turn up to see fair play and we sat them on rather, of necessity, tightly packed rows of chairs at one end of the room. It was a cold February day and as the morning wore on the room became rather stuffy, to relieve which somebody turned on the ceiling fans that drew air straight from the roof above and discharged it through grills that happened to be above the tenants' heads. When we came back from a lunch break not one of the tenants had returned. The cold air had evidently done its work and the case proceeded in a much quieter atmosphere.

On another occasion I was working in my City office when I heard a loud voice in the entrance hall asking to speak to the senior partner. Kenneth, who was also in the City office at that time as Surveyor to the Mercers' Company was, as I have said, at times a painfully reserved man. He must have heard the request also but he made no move. I therefore went out into the entrance hall of the small office which was all on one floor, to find the rather self important senior partner of a firm of City solicitors who looked at my evident youth with some disdain. This was one of those occasions however when my surname opened doors and when he heard it he became much more amenable. As a result we obtained a most interesting instruction to advise the Imperial Cancer Research Fund over its develop-ment of an extension of its headquarters in Lincolns Inn Fields. I was slightly concerned at one point that the Old Curiosity Shop was in danger of falling into the excavations, but all was well. Thereafter, I was able to be involved in some fascinating buildings, both in London and at the Fund's laboratories that were built on the northern outskirts. When inspecting the proposed site for the new laboratories I came upon a film shooting which involved a woman in period dress wading into a small lake. It was a cold morning and I was intrigued to note how many times the poor actress had to repeat the experience before the director was satisfied. As to the buildings, the sight that sticks in my mind is of rows of identical white rats in little compartments, inhaling cigarette smoke for all they were worth. I was assured that after a short time they become addicts and can not be taken off the treatment. But it was a long time ago and perhaps things are done differently nowadays.

Other activities that added variety were outside trusteeships and non-executive directorships to which I was invited and to which my partners agreed on the assumption that they were unlikely to do the firm any harm! The first of these invitations, which also led to by far my longest involvement, came in 1967 from the assets secretary to the Church Commissioners, whom I could hardly refuse as he was the main point of contact with our largest client. He was a trustee of the Royal Foundation of Grey Coat Hospital and as they were looking for additional trustees he asked me to join them, which I duly did. The trust is responsible for the Grey Coat Hospital girls' school in Westminster and Queen Anne's girl's school at Caversham. I did not know much about education, and still don't, but there were plenty of trustees and school governors who did. My contribution, apart from helping to direct the finances, was to apply such skills as I have to the extensive building programmes at both schools necessary to bring them up to modern requirements and to make them competitive in terms of building quality and the amenities provided. This involved, among other things, building squash courts, a swimming pool, two sports halls, music centre, arts centre and many new classrooms with, in Westminster, a completely new senior school on land acquired for the purpose. For the last twenty years of my Trusteeship I was invited to occupy the chair and I finally retired in 2002 after a very interesting time during which I had the pleasure of working with many unsung people who gave a great deal of voluntary and expert care and attention to the schools.

In the early seventies several similar tasks came along. One was from a property developer client in the City who invited me to join with my cousin Sam, who had a mutual horological interest with him, as a board member, which I did for a decade or so and which for a short time pitched me into the chair of the National Safe Deposit Company which had a fascinating structure extending to many levels beneath the city pavements. It was only a nominal job but it certainly added to the list of the more extraordinary buildings with which I had had the pleasure of being involved! I was amused to see that one of my predecessors in earlier years had been the man who subsequently became First Commissioner to both of my major clients. Small world! The developer was a remarkable man, short and stocky in stature and with a penetrating look from under large black eyebrows. He usually knew exactly what he was going to do but he enjoyed board meetings with his friends, at which he sometimes went through a semblance of indecision while he listened to our various opinions. Sometimes there were what appeared, on the surface, to be real problems of one sort or another that we might discuss at length before our chairman, who had a quite exceptional ability to do his homework from every conceivable angle, would suggest a solution. He was a very engaging man and friend.

Before I became a board member however I was the junior partner in the firm called in for various small jobs. One of these was to let a vacant floor in one of his office buildings. I duly presented my advice as to the rent that I thought should be quoted, when he asked to see my calculations. 'Your floor area is too little,' he said, 'Here, look at this' and passed over his own figures. After seeing them I said 'I think Sir your area includes that of the lavatories which are not, by the normal convention, regarded as useable space.' 'They use the lavatories, don't they?' he retorted. 'Well yes, they do.' 'Put them in then.' End of conversation! Fortunately he did not apply the same principle to the stairs.

Another early involvement was with the Salvation Army when I replaced one of my retiring partners on the Army's London

Advisory Board which met at their headquarters in Queen Victoria Street for the purpose of being briefed on current ideas and problems so that Board members could offer advice, where they could, from the benefit of their business or other experience. I learned to have great respect for the work done by the Army and for the people who do it. Later, I was asked to sit on the board of the Army's Housing Association, which I did for a few years and for as long as I could spare the time. It was very worthwhile work but I never really found it interesting and as there were board members who were expert in all aspects of housing I did not feel too guilty in giving way to others after a few years. Among my few testimonials I still have a certificate of Advisory Board membership for life, although I would now feel a bit of a fish out of water in taking this literally and actually turning up! The Army has some charming people but this was another meeting place where you felt that, while they expressed their gratitude for advice, they usually knew in advance what they were going to do. Sometimes this was the opposite of what the business minded board suggested because the priorities of the Army were, in some situations, of a more humane than business nature.

The Church Commissioners did a number of major developments with Lord Rayne's London Merchant Securities, on the usual arrangement where they provided the land and part of the finance and participated in rents and profits. I was involved in the Angel Centre scheme at the junction on the City and Pentonville Roads, and also in unscrambling the Commissioners' participation in an estate off Tottenham Court Road, after the developments had been completed and for the same reason that they withdrew from Paternoster and similar joint company arrangements elsewhere. I had already known Lord Rayne from the days when my firm acted for the Special Trustees of St Thomas' Hospital, of whom he was one. On the strength of this acquaintance he asked me to join the National Theatre Board, which he chaired, when the new building opened on the South Bank. My initial and particular task as a Board member was to try to help the administration over the many problems that occurred in getting the building completed and in dealing with a large list of post-completion snagging items. This involved trying to identify and agree responsibilities for faults and efforts to make various very complicated and innovative items of theatre machinery actually work! When one theatre critic commented upon an early production in the Olivier Theatre that it sounded as if the drum revolve was being pushed around by Chinese coolies, or some such expression, he was not to know that he was absolutely right, except that they were not Chinese! This was a fascinating assignment that lasted for seventeen years until I was embarrassed to find that I was the longest serving Board member; what time the Arts Minister thought that enough was enough and wrote me what I imagine must be the nicest sacking letter that anyone could expect. My chairman, in her kindness, had my name put on the complimentary ticket list for life and Jill and I are able to enjoy shows from time to time on terms that even country bumpkin pensioners can afford.

The appointment that naturally pleased me very much, because I never thought that one such as I would ever be considered, was to the Legal and General Main Board which met at the Society's headquarters in Queen Victoria Street. This was something completely new as I had had no involvement with the workings of a public company and there was a great deal to learn and understand. I found myself in a group of really friendly people all of whom were obviously at the tops of their chosen walks in life and experts in what they did. Throughout the twenty years of my involvement I sensed however that they never really did understand the workings of a privately owned partnership and I suppose I, despite my best efforts, never quite became a company man. It was though a most stimulating time, particularly when the chairman asked me to chair the committee that had to oversee, on the Board's behalf, the enormous programmes of property investment both within the Life Fund and also in the newly created Property Managed Fund.

Our first major investment turned out to be something of a disaster. With very large amounts of premium income to invest it was not always easy to find enough suitable investments. When therefore the Society was offered a large property portfolio it gave an opportunity to invest considerable funds in one transaction. The portfolio included some development situations that carried a degree of risk, but not beyond what, in the market of the time, was regarded as acceptable. A few months later however the market crashed in spectacular fashion and we found ourselves saddled with some large and suddenly very difficult property development situations which were only unscrambled after a lot of hard work. On the plus side, I was able to contribute to discussion about the large amounts of money still going out to developers on long term fixed interest mortgages, which enabled them in many cases to make substantial profits on the backs, so to speak, of the Society's policyholders and shareholders. From that point on the Board accepted that if a development was likely to be successful they should aim for a greater exposure to controlling the investment and the resulting profits rather than lending the funds on terms that enabled someone else to take most of the benefit. Under this policy we were able to take the investment lead in many substantial and profitable schemes throughout the country.

The old attitude to lending to developers, in the days before inflation was perceived to be a problem, was illustrated by the apocryphal story of an insurance company board being confronted by a mortgage manager who was proudly reporting a proposal to lend a large sum to a developer on interest of x per cent fixed for twenty years. 'That's no good to us,' was the response. 'We want security. Go back and fix it for forty years.' Which he did.

I had one other public company non-executive role with Haslemere Estates, originally a developer specializing in office conversion schemes, to which one of my partners had been independent valuer. After the Company had been taken over by the Dutch concern, Rodamco, a different firm was given the independent valuer role and my partner had, in any case, retired. I was free therefore to accept an invitation to join the board, a choice no doubt due to the fact that I was already familiar with many of the properties within the portfolio. As, however, a number of these were leased from clients of my firm I used frequently to have to spend parts of board meetings pacing the corridor outside, to avoid any conflict of interest. Subsequently, board meetings were held in Rotterdam which meant losing a whole day rather than an hour or two from my office. This did not matter much as I was by that time a semi-retired consultant to my firm and could afford the time. The round trips to Rotterdam did nevertheless become a little tedious, particularly during the time that Jill and I were making our home on the Isle of Wight. So after a time, when a new chief executive was appointed to replace the one who had recruited me, I took the opportunity to bow out. But not before one trip to Rotterdam for which I turned up as usual and made the journey to the flight departure gate. As I reached it I was greeted with a 'Good morning Mr Clutton'. 'How do you know my name?' I asked, to which the reply was 'Would you like to see the passenger list?' For the only time in my life I found myself the sole passenger. The stewardess, having found that I was familiar with the aircraft's flight safety procedures, was glad to be saved going

Our family at the time of my retirement. (L to R) Jonathan, Niall,
Owen, Gareth and Helen. Photograph by Niall Clutton.

through the usual routine. She then said 'Do you have young children?' I said 'You flatter me. I have several young grandchildren.' 'Then you had better relieve me of these,' she said and tipped the flight's allocation of boiled sweets into my open briefcase. One last bonus was that the crew did not bother to shut the cockpit door so that on this unique occasion I was able to see, through the cockpit, what the ground looks like as a plane comes in to land.

One more appointment, and an unusual one that also filled some of the time gaps that were appearing in my working day in the run down to retirement, was to the Royal Commission for the Exhibition of 1851. Until I was invited to it I had not known that such a body existed. I then found that the Great Exhibition had been almost unique among such events in making a

The earlier five of our nine grandchildren, George, Anna, William, Rafe and Toby, subsequently followed by Christopher, Jonathan, Finn and Rufus. Photograph by Niall Clutton.

considerable profit. The Commissioners exist to administer the land, property and monies left over from the event and to devote the income to provide postgraduate grants and scholarships, mostly for scientific or engineering research. Having served 'Commissioner' clients all my life, it was rather fun at last to be one myself! My specific task was to join one or two others on a finance committee, with a particular brief concerning the Commission's property holdings. There were other Commissioners and distinguished invitees who made up the committees that decided upon the merits of the award applications and research proposals. The full board met twice a year, when I found myself in the company of some pretty impressive people, each of whom were leaders in their various scientific and engineering fields and amongst whom I felt rather pedestrian! Once every other year we had a City livery hall dinner in the company of our President, the Duke of Edinburgh, who made the evening go with a swing with some amusing speechmaking after we had all seen presentations of the research projects of the current award holders, who also attended the dinners. I used to smile after these and other London dinners to watch the large chauffeur driven cars collecting the top brass, while the likes of me padded off to the nearest tube station, but consoling myself with the thought that at least I was, hopefully, getting some benefit from walking it off a bit.

For my last two years the firm was going through a bad property market and I therefore did a three day week as a consultant for remuneration roughly equal to that of my secretary, concentrating upon ensuring that my client relationships were passed on in a manner acceptable to them and to secure them to the firm. At around this time the RICS introduced what was called Continuous Professional Development, whereby all practising members are required to keep a diary of a minimum number of attendances at lectures, seminars and the like designed to ensure that their skills are kept up to date and that they are taking the trouble to be informed of matters relevant to their practice. I felt that I had been teaching myself new techniques and advising clients upon how they would be affected by new legislation throughout my working life and that, in my declining years, I hardly needed to be lectured. I failed therefore to keep a diary that would have passed the random inspection procedure that was set up in order to try to ensure compliance. I am glad to say that I was never put to that particular test. My other creeping worry was that all sorts of wires and terminals were being run round the office to take new equipment with which to prepare us for the twenty first century.

In due course the wires and terminals appeared on my office skirting board but I am glad to say that in my room the equipment never materialized. One needs a little luck in life!

CHAPTER 14

And Afterwards

FOR TEN YEARS after my father in law died in 1983 Jill's mother lived in our annexe until her own death a decade later. While therefore the family were gradually leaving home we did not think of doing so ourselves until I finally stopped work in 1994. By that time our home of thirty three years, which we had watched rising from the ground with such excitement all that time ago, really was too big. I used to open bedroom doors last thing at night to let the air circulate, thinking of the days when they were alive with children's voices, and then shut them again in the morning to keep the dogs out. It was time to think of a move.

On my retirement from the partnership in 1992 I received back the partnership capital that had been accumulated from years of forgoing income and this we invested in a small holiday house at Ventnor, on the Isle of Wight. The idea was to have a base for ourselves and also somewhere where the family, with their own young children, could holiday inexpensively. We had taken breaks on the Island on several occasions and had grown quite fond of its relaxed charm, plus the feeling one had of leaving mainland cares behind when crossing the Solent. We thus had somewhere to which to go when we sold our home at Chailey in September 1995 and while we looked for a new, but smaller, house in Sussex. What we did not anticipate was that the search would take almost two years, as we inspected and rejected well over a hundred houses. Nothing that we liked came up in Chailey so in desperation we eventually settled on our present home which, although only in the next village, is nevertheless some four miles distant from where we were.

As a surveyor, I at last followed the maxim of 'location; location; location!' The position is rural and peaceful, with the noisiest traffic being the occasional farm tractor. We have a large enough and interesting garden, in which the house is well positioned with plenty of room all round it, complete with a small paddock and an even smaller piece of woodland and views across the valley of the River Ouse and to the South Downs above Lewes. The house was built in the nineteen thirties as a two up, two down gardener's cottage. This had been extended by several minor additions but the whole had been sadly neglected for many years. Our predecessors seem to have been happy to live with archaic plumbing, heating and wiring, plus woodworm in the attics and mice almost everywhere! When the south west rains hit the exposed front door they came straight through it and ran down inside! Our builders had a great time unearthing the skeletons; literally so when removal of the covering to a light switch revealed two mummified mice facing each other in a position of apparent supplication, rather like the heads on canopic jars regarding each other for all eternity in some Egyptian tomb. The water main was of lead, furred up internally to rather less than the diameter of a pencil. The plumber assumed that the former owners must either have bathed together or on alternate days, from the time that he estimated it would take the storage tank to fill.

But the location was right, the structure was sound and the house had potential. After three years of on and off building work we now have a comfortable home that is quite large enough for the two of us, but not so big that we risk exhaustion in our old age by too many of the family staying at once! Our son Gareth and his wife Fiona live ten minutes away in a large house that can take their three children and any overnight overflow from ours. With their larger establishment they are also very generous in hosting the whole family on special occasions; an excellent arrangement as seen by those who are starting to slow down a bit! Work to our Barcombe house has included almost complete renewal of all services, all windows and external doors, plus new kitchen and bathrooms and a large conservatory to give us an extra family/living room. We now keep our fingers crossed that nothing should wear out until after we do!

While our second son and his family are the nearest to where we live, the rest of the family are no more than an hour's drive away, other than our daughter, Helen, and her husband who are a bit further in Dorset, but still quite accessible. Our eldest son, Owen, has not married but the others all have children and we are proud grandparents to a granddaughter and eight grandsons, all of whom we see often. We are thus greatly blessed and feel fortunate to be so rich in the things that matter most in life.

It is not easy to retire. The transition from responsibilities and involvement to freedom but also powerlessness can be difficult and, if one does not recognize and resist it, depressing. When I was approaching this unemployed state I became more observant of its effect upon others and how they faced it. When a retired colleague came in to the office I tried to show that I had time for him and to discuss the affairs of the firm in the same way that I would have done when he was in harness. It was nevertheless slightly embarrassing to be aware of how different our relationship now was. A few people would drift in rather too often and some friends would protest rather too much about how much they were still in demand. Our partnership did not have the ability to allow much in the way of 'perks' to those who retired but we did, until times hit a bad patch and we could no longer afford it, give them their office cars on retirement and some continued to use their former secretaries for correspondence, typing tax returns and the like.

Seeing all this, I was determined not to impose at all on my hard pressed continuing partners once I had left. Well beforehand I acquired my first word processor and am now on to the third. I would not pretend to be an expert and the machine still displays exasperating quirks from time to time, but I can now at least use more than the proverbial two fingers and it is quite satisfying to be able, when needed, to produce letters of near office quality. My working life was helped very much by two really excellent secretaries and that does spoil one.

It seems to me that retirement also requires a change of attitude and I believe that the sooner this can be brought about the sooner one can enjoy the new status, or rather lack of status. When friends have been kind enough to comment that retirement suits me and ask the secret I answer that one just needs to realize that one is no longer important, if indeed one ever was. It is relatively easy for me because I was brought up in a happy but fairly impoverished environment and most of our friends are from similar, unremarkable backgrounds. While Jill and I have had a good life with some good holidays, neither of us have hankered after expensive pursuits or hobbies – except perhaps for my short spells of sailing – still less for the company of high society, so what we have never really wanted we certainly now do not miss! I still attend my surveyors' dining clubs in London, plus the occasional lunch with old friends, and it is always good to see everyone, but it is also good not to have to make the journey to London too often!

When I recently took up daily cycle riding, after a lapse of forty years, as a supplement to exercise in the garden, our former Rector, now also in retirement, said 'Second childhood is a wonderful thing!' and I know what he means. Actually, I had forgotten the pleasure of cycling and of riding along quiet country lanes with your head rather higher than it is in a car and with both the ability and freedom to look over the hedgerows and to enjoy the view. Our son Niall is a keen cyclist of the head down, fifty mile spin before lunch, variety and I owe to him, plus the generosity of all the family, the choice and presentation of a machine ideally designed for the older and slower cyclist. I did not realize how slow until his two sons, staying complete with bikes, offered to accompany me on a ride. We no sooner set off than they disappeared, but were kind enough to slow down as we did the circuit a second time.

If I have not said much about our family it is because I do not feel that it is for me to talk about their lives. That is their prerogative and I would not intrude. I hope it is clear from what I have said how highly we regard all of them; they are indeed the purpose of and the reward for our lives. At the time of writing this we have just been presented with our ninth grandchild and eighth grandson, the second son of our third son Jonathan and his wife Lisa. Niall and his wife Helen have two boys and our daughter Helen and her husband David another two boys; Gareth and his wife Fiona started the two boys precedent, but after having our granddaughter. Although our first son Owen is not married, he is thus in the fortunate position of having no lack of enjoyment of the company of his niece and nephews and is much in demand, particularly for outings to pantomimes and the like, as a very welcome and entertaining uncle.

Should one sum up a little history such as this by asking, as did Wells's giant in 'The Food of the Gods', sitting on his tree stump and watching the little people scurrying about below him on their daily business, 'What's it all for?' I suppose that when you are retired there is time to reflect on it all in a way for which there is less time during a busy life. I did not so much choose to be a surveyor as follow the wishes of others. Nevertheless, while there have been dull and humdrum tasks to be done, the surveyor's work that fell to me was mostly of a kind that made me feel that it was worthwhile and productive and I have certainly been proud to be part of such a stimulating and friendly profession. Someone has to manage property assets and, while the management of property estates may, to the deal making entrepreneur for instance, seem routine or downright dull, the work does have its satisfying aspects, as I have tried to show. Our efforts to foster and maintain good relations between landlord and tenant and to make their premises such as they would wish, although not always to everyone's satisfaction, did, I think, improve the quality of life for many people. Time spent talking to people in their own homes, farms or places of work was generally worth while, even though one could not always satisfy all demands.

As to whether it was worth it, it paid the bills and saw our family through from play school to polytechnic or university, which is as much as I ever asked for. Looked at as a business, the rewards were probably inadequate for the risks of twenty or so equity partners employing a staff of well over four hundred, not to mention commitments to the costs of offices and equipment, and running the ever present possibility of bankruptcy in a bad year. Many a modest country estate agency, in the misguided scramble by the institutions to purchase outlets through which to sell their financial services, made far more money than we did from years of hard work and considerable responsibility. One would say, yes, but at least we remained in control of our businesses and self employment. But then so did some of the estate agency principals when the institutions realized their mistake and the original owners of the businesses were able to buy them back at something like a tenth of the sums for which they had sold them!

I was amused not long ago to hear of a conversation between Gareth and an administrator to one of our clients who had evidently assumed that the rewards of the senior partners were at least three times what they actually were. No wonder they were always pressing for fee scale pruning! In fact, estate management is not usually a high margin activity but, against this, the income is reasonably predictable. Our problem, which was an historical one, lay in having a large agricultural management service that was an integral and unavoidable part of our work for the major clients on whom, for many years, the business was almost wholly dependant, but which often made little overall profit, while comprising almost half of the partnership manpower. This was the situation that many of us had been used to for most of our working lives and we regarded it as the price for the managements that the same clients entrusted to us for urban estates. It did however dilute profitability when compared with the majority of our competitors who had no agricultural side; still more so in comparison with the mainly commercial agency practices, which is why my generation tried so hard to diversify into these areas.

As time went by, our younger urban intake were less prepared to spend their lives supporting agriculture and, as a result, we lost some promising young partners. During my time in the hot seat I tried to do two things to cope with this situation. The first was to lower the partner retirement age from sixty five to sixty so that younger partners might see the prospect of promotion to be more open, while providing the right, for a period, to allow those partners immediately affected to work on as well paid consultants until age sixty five. This had an advantage for some in the upper age bracket in that tax relief on pension provision, which all equity partners had to make from their own pockets, was substantially better for them as employees than it had been when they were self employed.

The second change, which was much more difficult, was to persuade partners to accept that, if the firm was to be able to

*'Darby and Joan', from the Barcombe Village photographic Millennium
Record of inhabitants in the year 2000.*

attract the commercial people that everyone agreed that we
needed, their share of profits must have some relationship to the
earnings of the branch of the firm's work in which they
practiced. This caused some protest, even though the variation
in the shares was little more than a token one. It did however
make a start into a change that was inevitable if the firm was to
be able to keep and adequately motivate those upon whom its
future profitability depended. Since I left, this essential
refinement of partnership profit sharing has, I believe, been
taken much further. Perhaps if it had been possible to be so
forward looking a generation ago our efforts to expand our
commercial operations might have proceeded more quickly!
However, while agricultural partners were as keen as anyone
that the firm should be more profitable, some of them were less

keen on the implication that those profits should accrue more fairly to those who earned them! As we had expanded after the war, the custom of equal sharing between equal equity partners had for many years had to be modified as between senior and junior and also between those working in Central London and others in charge of country branches and working in provincial towns. In the spirit of democracy however, each partner, irrespective of his share of the profits, had one vote in the running and organization of the business. With almost half the head count at the time being in agriculture or other provincial work it was, not surprisingly, difficult to make much more than a token reallocation of profit shares in order to reflect a need for different emphasis.

Since my retirement I understand that the firm has been able to move further in adjustment of rewards to meet the inescapable lessons of the recruitment market within the profession and I like to think that, with these and other progressive changes, the firm is now much better placed to earn its living in the future. Although a retiring partner ceases to have any financial or other involvement with his former partnership, it is hard to break the habit of a lifetime's concern for its welfare. Our sons and our son in law all have interesting work in different areas and there has not been any assumption, as there was for my brother and for me, that we should naturally go into what was regarded as the family business. Nevertheless I feel very happy that Gareth, on his own decision and after trying a few other jobs, decided to make his future with the firm and to keep alive the Clutton name within it. It is an even greater source of pleasure to know that he is earning the respect of both clients and partners in doing such a good job. Long may it continue!

Watching the business and political world now from our country retreat, I can't help feeling fortunate to have been working in the second half of the last century. Not only did the trains usually run on time but it was easier to feel respect for those in positions of business or political leadership than it sometimes is today. Of course, some of the great weren't great and some good were far from that, but by and large it was possible to assume that those at the top were honest, competent and dedicated to the point that they were not just there only for as long as they were voted increasingly disproportionate financial rewards. At the lower level, our family farmhouse doors were seldom locked or the windows closed. The only larceny that I can recall was a mysterious shrinking of the contents of the whisky decanter on the dining room sideboard that we eventually found to be caused by the postman who, delivering the letters at a time in the morning when the house was unoccupied because of the station and school run, was unable to resist the opportunity for a spot of refreshment. In a world where we have to be vigilant for not only theft and fraud within but also terrorism from without, one can only be concerned for the conditions in which our grandchildren will have to seek the fulfilment, security and happiness that we as children had no cause to doubt. I expect this has been a common cry from the older among us in all generations. Certainly, when I am enjoying the company of the family they all seem pretty positive and that is heartening.

As an aside, and reverting to the postman, he was an elderly man and he came down our lane on his bicycle. Any post that was readable was always read before we received it and I would be told as he arrived, for example, 'Your rugby match on Saturday has been cancelled. The card is with the letters.' One day he was complaining about the state of his boots. I still had my naval issue square bashing boots and asked him if he would like them. When I dug them out of storage I found that the toes had curled upwards to a considerable degree but he bore them off gladly. I was amused afterwards to see that he was wearing them, apparently suffering no discomfort from the fact that his toes were pointing Heavenwards. This however was at least better than the old lady who used to walk from the village to deliver telegrams by hand, always in carpet slippers with pompoms on the toes. Another oddity was the milkman who called once the trips to the dairy were no more. He delivered green or red topped bottles and one day gave us the wrong colour. When this was pointed out he confessed that he was colour blind and could not tell the difference, relying entirely on the bottles being placed on the right part of the float, which on this occasion they had not been. He eventually disappeared to hospital suffering from tannin poisoning from accepting some twenty to thirty cups of tea on his rounds from customers whom he did not like to offend.

We were of course very lucky. In our relative ignorance of the world around us we did not know how lucky. Today we are informed day by day of such terrible injustice, inequality and bestiality of man to man that it literally does not bear thinking about because we are so helpless to do much about it. We send what little we can to relief organizations and pray that some good may come from evil. I am conscious that we and our family and friends live in a privileged strata of a privileged country and I ponder the lottery whereby so many are born to draw a much shorter straw. My own mother had two children, a boy and a girl between my sister Shirley and me, who did not survive the first twenty-four hours of life. I think of them, and particularly I suppose of the elder brother whose life, together with my own and that of my siblings, would have been so different had he lived. My father often spoke of the two missing babies. My mother never did, probably because the anguish of losing two in a row must have been too painful. Her only sign came on my twenty first birthday when she sent a card to me at my London digs saying 'The day you were born and survived was the happiest of my life.'

So, to me at least it is a puzzle that our chances in life are so different. While I fully accept and believe the Christian Gospel I find it odd that our teaching seems to be relatively silent concerning those millions who have no access to that teaching or whose lives are either cut short or so blighted that they also lack instruction. I do believe however that, contrary to what some scientists like to think, the universe is infinite and beyond our understanding and that the same must apply to its Creator and guiding intelligence. There is a hymn in which the writer chides us for putting limits to God. I take consolation in the belief that there are no limits and that, in that infinity, there are loving answers to all in life that assails and perplexes us.

It is against that background that I am so grateful for a happy, fulfilling and interesting life, knowing that so many are not so fortunate. I just hope that it will go on for as long as may be permitted, both so that Jill and I can continue to enjoy each other's company and also so that we can watch the family thrive and our grandchildren grow up – or at least as far up we may be given the time to observe! I can think of no more enjoyable and rewarding way of passing the time that is left to us. It seems ages ago now that, embarking on my first solo property inspection as the proud representative of the Commissioners for Crown Lands, I was greeted by one of their tenants looking me up and down and saying 'Aren't you too young for this sort of thing?' Now I feel that, moored so to speak in calmer waters away from the bustle of the main tideway, there is some comfort in being too old!

Index